Ready, Set, Bead!

25 quick & easy stitching projects

Kalmbach Books
21027 Crossroads Circle
Waukesha, Wisconsin 53186
www.JewelryAndBeadingStore.com

Published in 2017
20 21 19 18 17 1 2 3 4 5

Manufactured in China

ISBN: 978-1-62700-357-5
EISBN: 978-1-62700-358-2

Editor: Erica Barse
Book Design: Lisa Bergman
Proofreader: Dana Meredith
Photographer: William Zuback

Library of Congress Control Number: 2016943704

Ready, Set, Bead!

25 quick & easy stitching projects

Jane Danley Cruz

Waukesha, WI

Contents

Introduction

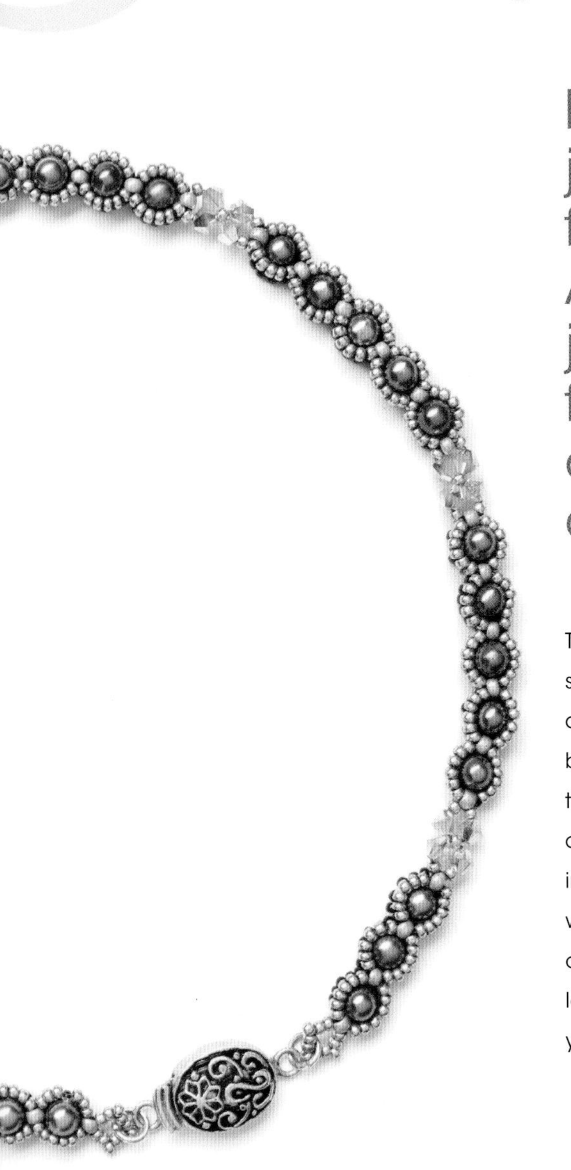

For me, finding the right jewelry is simply a matter of finding the time to make it. And since I love to make jewelry, I'm always trying to find an hour or so at the end of the day to sit down, relax, and stitch!

The projects in this book are my All-Star lineup for jewelry that can be stitched in four hours or less. Some of these are seasoned MVPs and some are promising rookies, but all of them are relatively easy. The chapters are broken down by the approximate time it takes for a beginning beader to complete a project. For example, each project in Chapter 1 can be completed in an hour or less; each project in Chapter 2 can be completed in two hours or less, and so on. The projects also get a little more involved with each chapter, progressing from flat to three dimensional, and one component to multiple components, etc. However, even if you are just learning to bead, you can start with a project in Chapter 4 just as easily as you can make a project in Chapter 1; it will just take longer to complete.

uction

Here's the warning section: I stitch with extremely tight tension. So tight, in fact, that I've given myself tendonitis in my left hand and tennis elbow in my right arm. Most of my projects include directions telling you to "snug up the beads." When I snug up my beads, my elbow twinges. I power through because tension is the key to professional-looking and long-lasting beadwork. However, I advise you to take a few short breaks during an hour of beading to flex your fingers, shrug your shoulders, and massage your forearms. Also, give your eyes a break and focus for 15–20 seconds on something across the room or out the window. The longer you bead, the more important this is for you. If I'm working on a project for several hours, I can generally count on my family to provide a distraction every 20–30 minutes, but if not, I set a timer so I force myself to take short breaks. Not only is it easier on my hands, arms, and neck, but I'm that much more invigorated to get back to my beading.

Since time seems to be the one thing we all have less and less of these days, it's important that you spend your free time doing things you enjoy. For me, making jewelry to wear or to give to friends as gifts is one of the most enjoyable, relaxing things I do for myself. I hope the same is true for you. Enjoy!

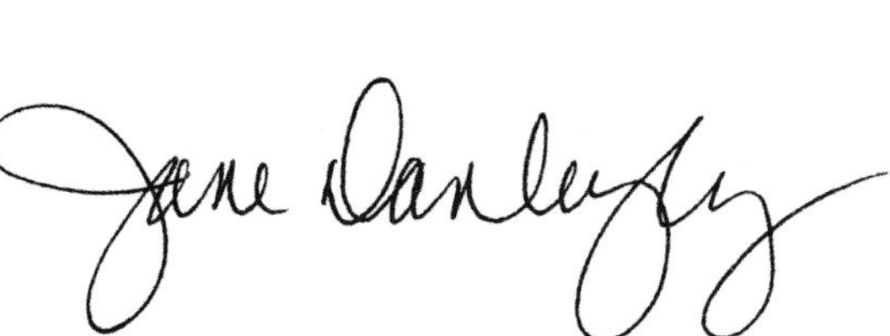

Basics

Beading Tools and Materials

To begin, you'll need a few common pliers, findings, and thread.

Seed Beads

Seed beads are available in an assortment of shapes and sizes, ranging from smaller than 1mm to larger than 6mm. Size is indicated by a number, followed by the (pronounced "aught") symbol, alternatively written as º. The higher the number, the smaller the bead.

I've used seed beads in many different shapes, including **bugle beads**, **Minos beads**, **drop beads**, **Rizzos**, **O-beads**, and **dagger beads**. I've also used a few two-hole beads: **SuperDuos**, **DiamonDuos**, **Tila beads**, and **two-hole cabochons**.

Seed beads can be bought in hanks, tubes, or bags. Czech seed beads are often sold by the hank, a bundle of 12 20-in. (51cm) strands. Beads sold in tubes or bags are usually sold by weight, measured in grams. I've listed them in this book according to the most common way the beads are sold.

Other Beads

I love **pearls**, which are showcased in this book, along with round and bicone **crystals**, **fire-polished beads**, **gemstone beads**, and **glass beads**. These larger beads help speed up the stitching process while at the same time adding plenty of interest to your jewelry.

I've even used some **cabochons** (a stone or crystal with a flat face and no hole) and **rivolis**. Be sure to choose quality beads from your local bead store, and play with different colors and finishes as you like to customize your jewelry.

Findings

Findings are components, usually made of metal, used to finish, connect, space, or embellish jewelry. Vendors may use the term for all metal jewelry-making components, or they may use it for specific items, such as clasps.

Clasps finish and connect the ends of necklaces and bracelets and should enhance the overall design of your piece. When choosing a clasp, try to keep the size proportionate to your jewelry; a casual and lightweight necklace may be quickly and easily fastened with a lobster claw clasp, but a chunky bracelet might warrant a larger toggle or box clasp.

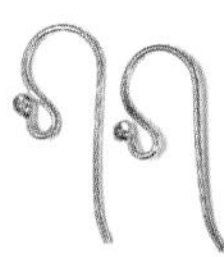

Earring wires slide through pierced ears or clamp onto earlobes, providing a loop or base for attaching earring components. They are available in a wide range of styles and many different metals and finishes. All have simple and decorative options.

Crimp ends are used to finish cord and ribbon strands. They compress or fold over the ends of the strands to hold them in place and provide loops for attaching clasps or other components.

Jump rings are tiny circles of wire, preferably with flush ends that close securely. They are used to link components, including clasps and strands. Most jump rings are round, but oval, square, and other shapes are also available. **Split rings** look like tiny key rings. Made from fine-gauge wire, split rings offer the security of soldered jump rings, but are more flexible in their use, since closed loops or soldered jump rings can be attached to them.

Thread and Cord

Fireline is a fishing line that is very popular as a beading thread. Made from a parallel filament gel-spun polyethylene called Dyneema that has been bonded to form a single-ply thread, Fireline is very strong and thin, it doesn't stretch, and it resists fraying. It comes in three colors: crystal (white), flame green, and smoke (dark gray). The smoke-colored Fireline has a dark residue which can get on hands and beads if the line isn't cleaned or conditioned before use. It comes in a range of thicknesses, labeled by break weight. Because of its strength and thinness, Fireline is great for stitching, especially with large beads or beads with sharp edges, like crystals. However, Fireline can still be cut by sharp bead edges. **Leather cord** is used for stringing pendants or knotted to produce flexible necklaces or bracelets.

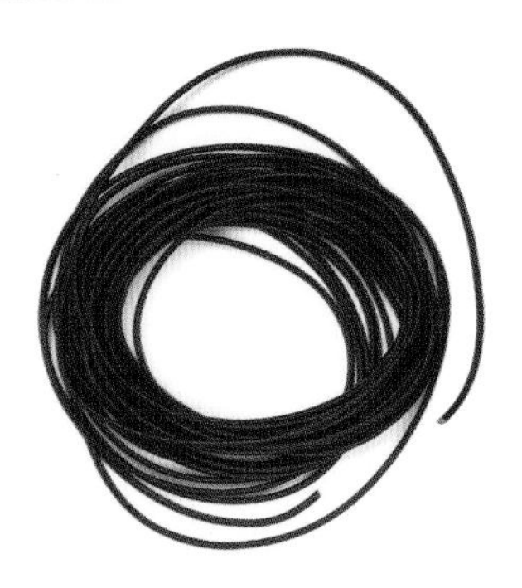

Tools

Beading needles are used for off-loom stitches and loomwork. Unlike sewing needles, the eye of a beading needle is almost as narrow as the shaft. Both Japanese and English beading needles are available, with the English needles being more flexible than the Japanese. The needles are numbered, and most frequently found in sizes #10–#16. The thinner the needle, the higher the needle number.

Pliers are used for holding, bending, and shaping wire and for opening and closing loops and jump rings. **Chainnose pliers** have flat jaws used to bend and shape wire and open and close jump rings. **Flatnose** and **bentnose pliers** are close relatives of **chainnose pliers**, featuring the same smooth inner jaws to help grasp wire or components without leaving marks. **Split-ring pliers** make it easier to open split rings without damaging your fingernails. The bent tip slides between the layers of the ring, holding them apart as you add components.

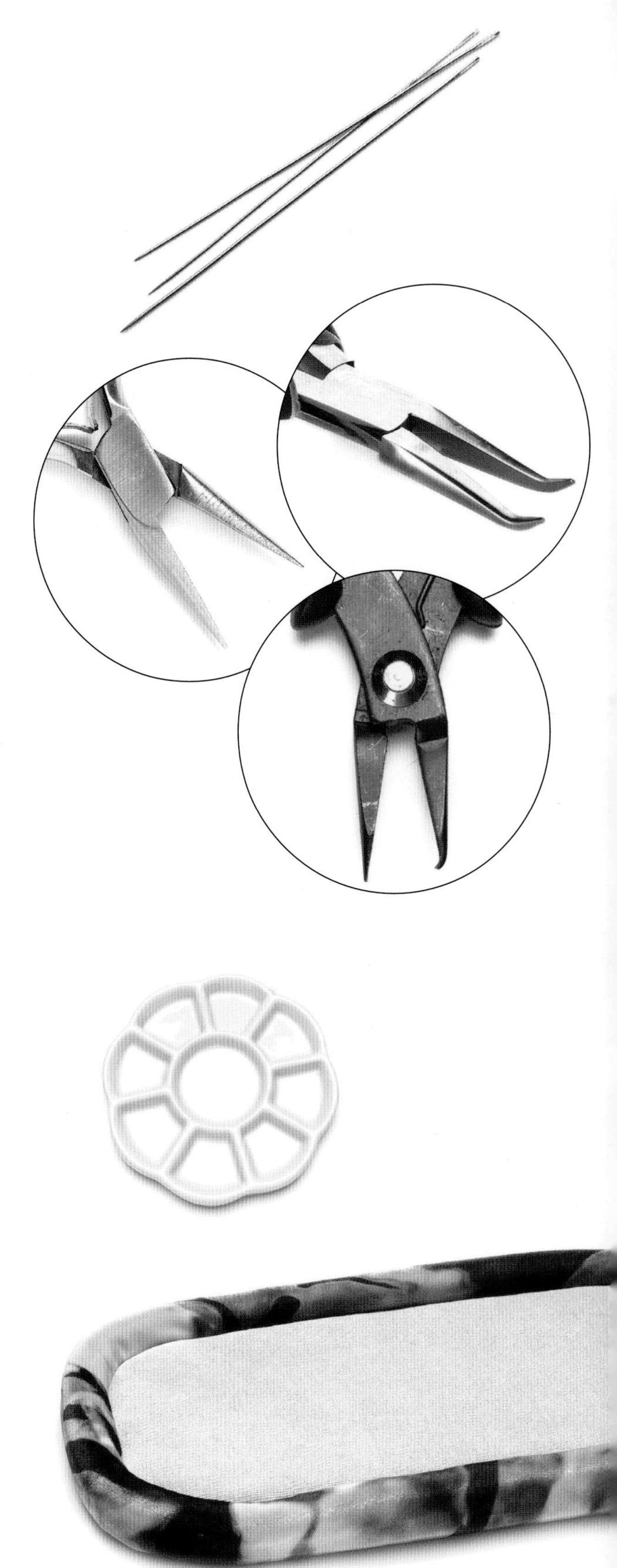

Other Items

Bead mats or **bead boards** are usually made of a soft or nubbed fabric, such as Vellux, and are used as a work surface for beading because their surface texture stops the beads from rolling away. **Bead dishes** are helpful for coralling tiny seed beads.

A **task lamp** makes it easier to see your work as you bead.

Beading Techniques

Use this section as a reference if you need a refresher on common beading techniques.

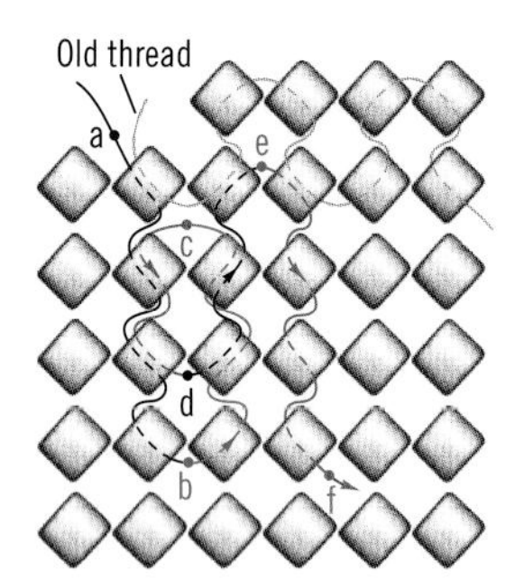

Ending and Adding Thread

To end a thread, sew back through the last few rows or rounds of beadwork, following the thread path of the stitch and tying two or three half-hitch knots (see "Half-hitch knot") between beads as you go. Sew through a few beads after the last knot, and trim the thread. To add a thread, sew into the beadwork several rows or rounds prior to the point where the last bead was added, leaving a short tail. Follow the thread path of the stitch, tying a few half-hitch knots between beads as you go, and exit where the last stitch ended. Trim the short tail.

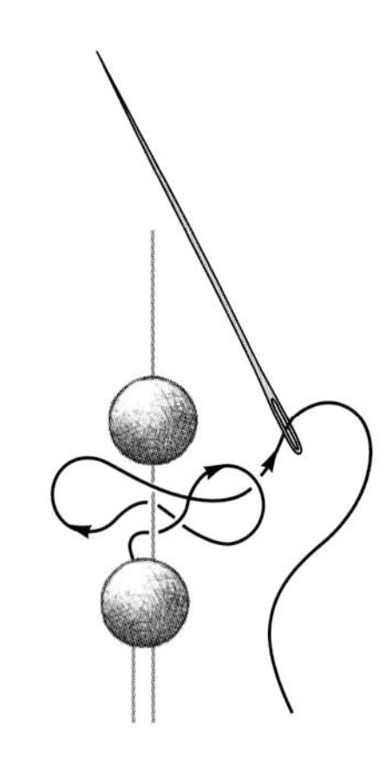

Half-Hitch Knot

Pass the needle under the thread between two beads. A loop will form as you pull the thread through. Cross over the thread between the beads, sew through the loop, and pull gently to draw the knot into the beadwork.

Overhand Knot

Make a loop at the end of the thread. Pull the short tail through the loop, and tighten.

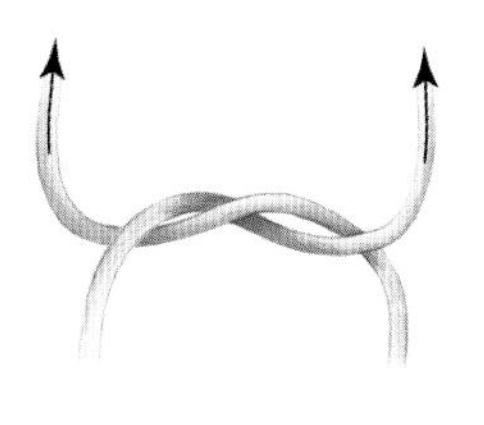

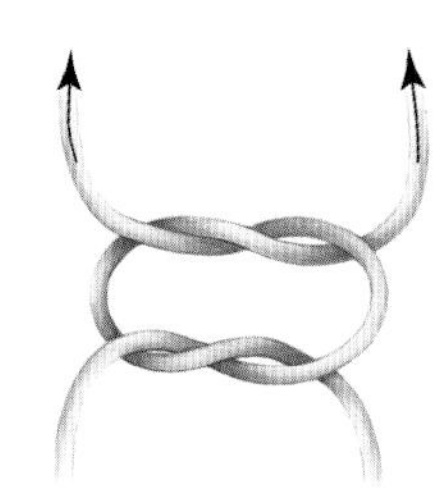

Square Knot

Cross the left-hand end of the thread over the right, and bring it around and back up.

Cross the end that is now on the right over the left, go through the loop, and pull both ends to tighten.

Attaching a Stop Bead

Use a stop bead to secure beads temporarily when you begin stitching. Pick up the stop bead, leaving the desired length tail. Sew through the stop bead again in the same direction, making sure you don't split the thread inside the bead. If desired, sew through the bead one more time for added security.

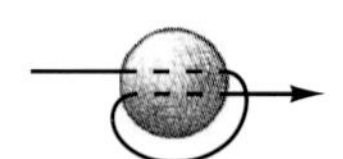

Opening and Closing Loops and Jump Rings

1 Hold a loop or a jump ring with two pairs of pliers, such as chainnose, flatnose, or bentnose pliers.

2 To open the loop or jump ring, bring the tips of one pair of pliers toward you, and push the tips of the other pair away from you.

3 Reverse step 2 to close the open loop or jump ring.

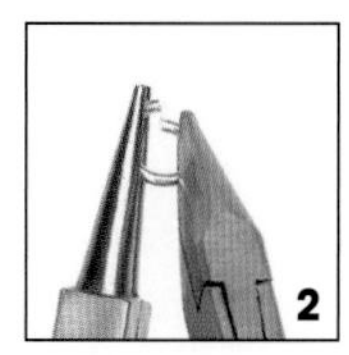

Opening Split Rings

Slide the hooked tip of split-ring pliers between the two overlapping wires.

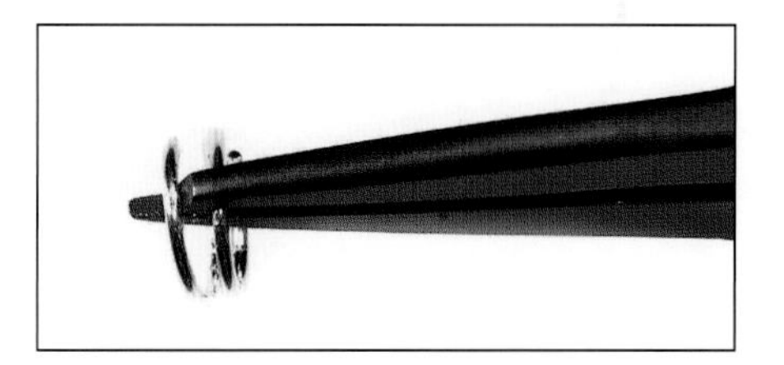

Crimping

Use a crimp end on the end of leather cord to attach a clasp. Slide the crimp end into place, and squeeze it firmly with chainnose pliers to flatten it.

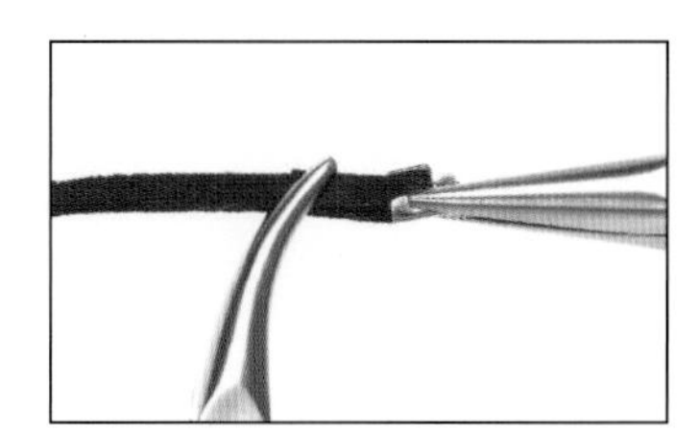

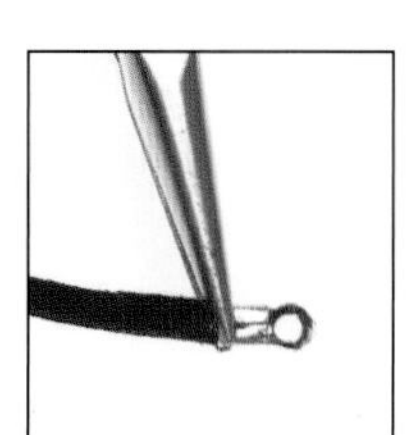

1 HOUR *Projects*

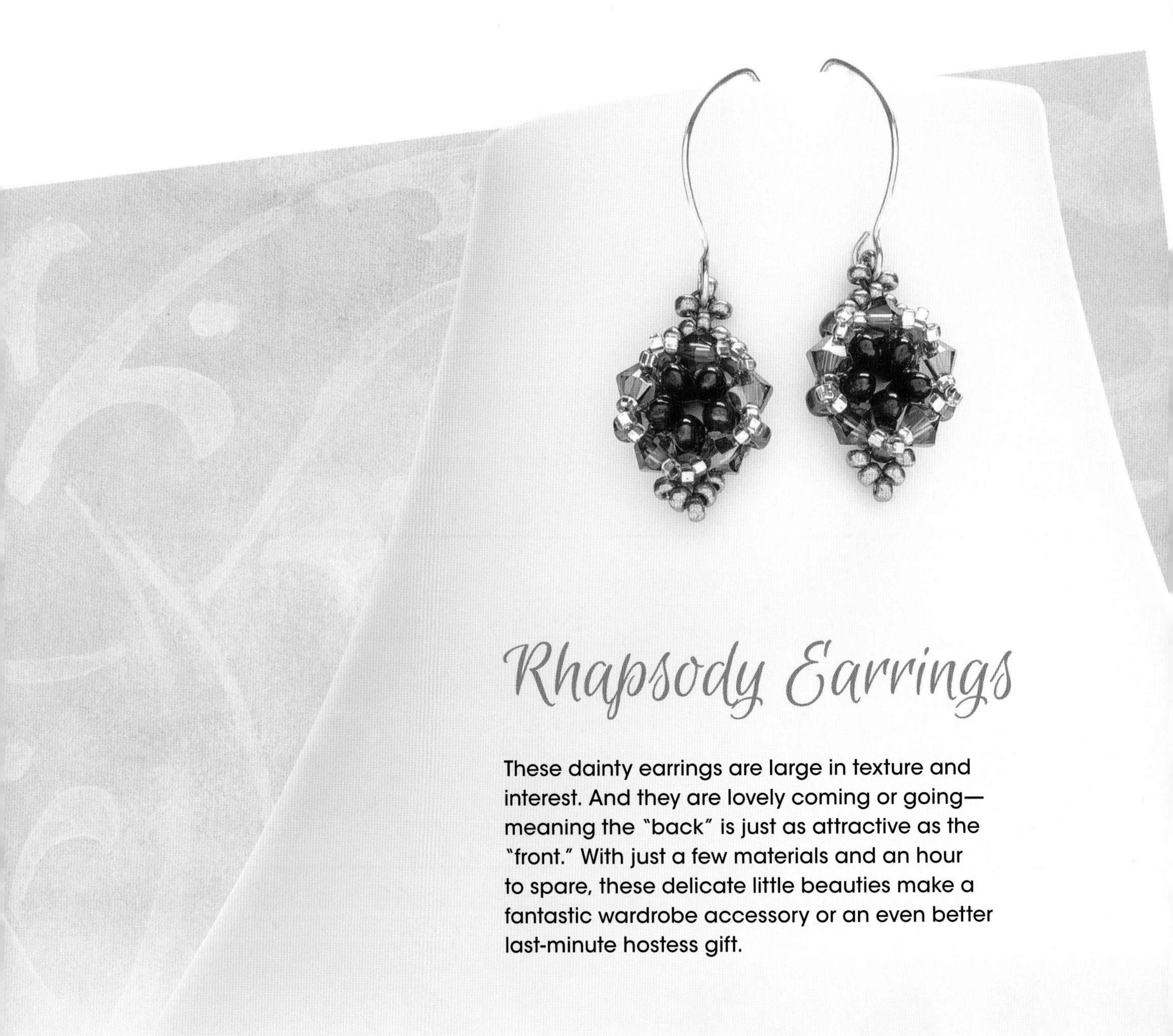

Rhapsody Earrings

These dainty earrings are large in texture and interest. And they are lovely coming or going—meaning the "back" is just as attractive as the "front." With just a few materials and an hour to spare, these delicate little beauties make a fantastic wardrobe accessory or an even better last-minute hostess gift.

SUPPLIES

- **10** 4mm bicone crystals
- **10** Rizzo beads
- 1g 8º seed beads
- 1g 11º seed beads
- 1g 15º seed beads
- Pair of earring wires
- Beading needle #10
- Fireline, 6 lb. test
- **2** pairs of chainnose pliers

a

Earrings

1. On a comfortable length of thread, pick up five Rizzo beads and sew through the beads again, leaving a 6-in. (15cm) tail. Tie a square knot (Basics, p. 12) with the working thread and the tail **(photo a)**.

2. Pick up an 11º seed bead and sew through the next Rizzo **(photo b)**. Repeat this stitch four more times to complete the round. Step up through the first 11º added in this step **(photo c)**.

3. Pick up an 11º, an 8º seed bead, and an 11º. Sew through the next 11º in the previous round **(photo d)**. Repeat to complete the round, and step up through the first 11º and 8º added in this step **(photo e)**. You're working on the back of your piece in this step. When you work with a firm tension, the beads added in this step force the Rizzos to sort of stand at attention in the center front.

4. Pick up a 4mm bicone crystal and sew through the next 8º in the previous round **(photo f)**. Repeat to complete the round. Retrace the thread path through the beads in this step using a firm tension, and step up through the first 4mm added in this step.

5. Pick up three 15º seed beads and sew through the next 4mm **(photo g)**. The 15ºs will sit on top of the 8ºs added in step 3 on the front of your work. Repeat to complete the round, but do not step up. Instead, exit the nearest 4mm.

6. Working on the back of the earring, sew through the nearest 8º **(photo h)**. Pick up five 11ºs and sew through the 8º again in the same direction to form a small loop **(photo i)**. Sew through the first two 11ºs in the loop, skip the next 11º, and sew through the following two 11ºs **(photo j)**. Continue through the 8º again and snug up the thread so the skipped 11º pops out

(photo k). Retrace the thread path and continue through the next 4mm, 8º, 4mm, and 8º **(photo l)**.

7. Pick up five 11ºs, skip the next 4mm, and sew through the next 8º. Sew through all the 4mms and 8ºs around the ring and continue through the first three 11ºs added in this step **(photo m)**.

8. Pick up three 11ºs and sew through the 11º your thread exited at the start of this step **(photo n)** to form a small loop. Retrace the thread path through the loop several times and end the threads (Basics).

9. Open the loop of an earring wire (Basics) and attach the small loop created in step 8. Close the loop.

10. Make a second earring.

l

m

n

If these earrings are too dainty for you, try one of the following options:

• Use fancier or more elaborate earring wires.

• Make two components and join them as follows: For the second component, in step 8, pick up an 11º, sew through the skipped 11º from step 6 on the first component, pick up an 11º, and work step 8 as written. This is a simple way to make a bolder statement to suit your personal style.

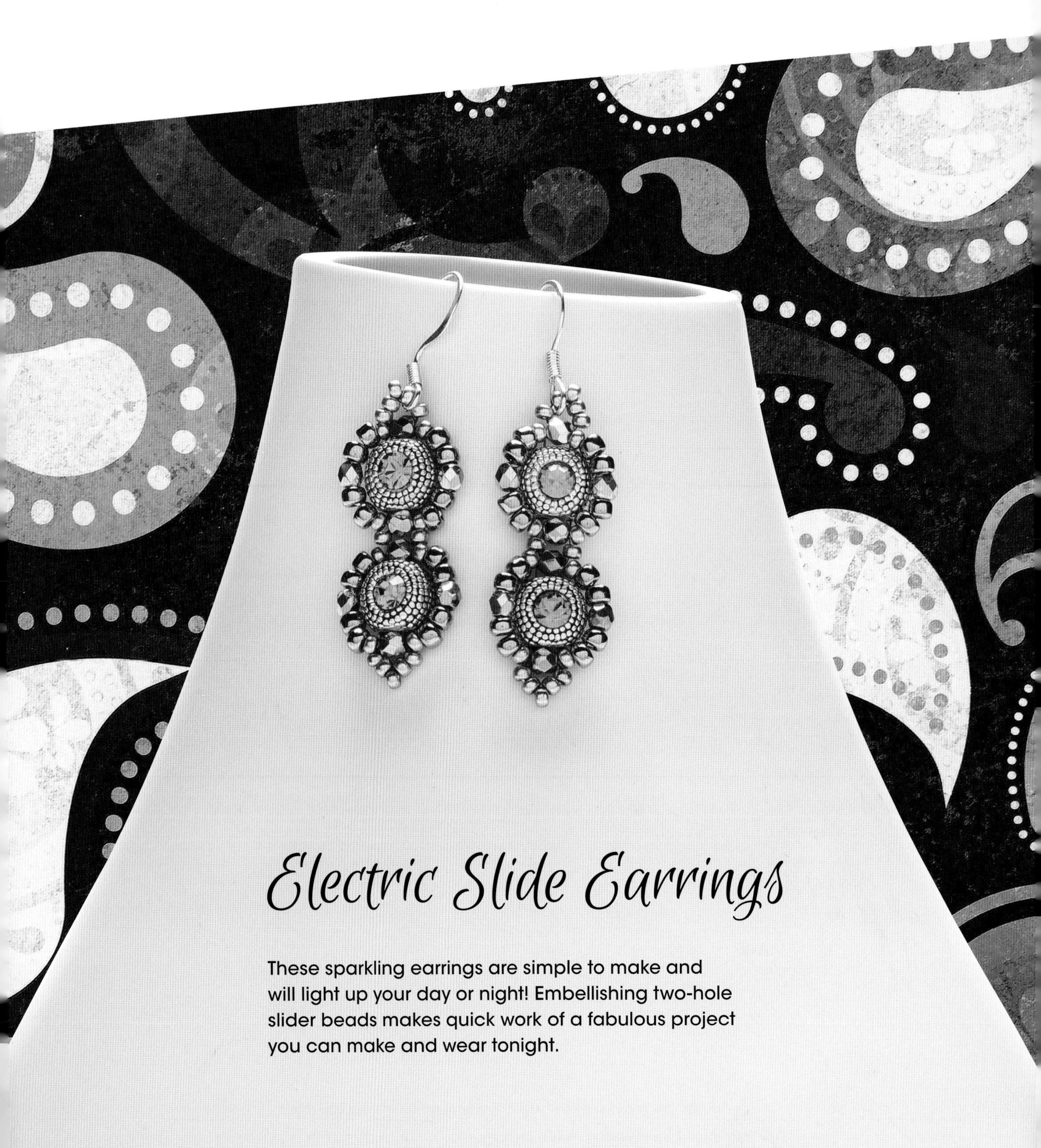

Electric Slide Earrings

These sparkling earrings are simple to make and will light up your day or night! Embellishing two-hole slider beads makes quick work of a fabulous project you can make and wear tonight.

SUPPLIES

- **4** 8mm 2-hole slider beads
- **16** 3mm fire-polished beads
- 1g $8^{\underline{o}}$ seed beads
- 1g $11^{\underline{o}}$ seed beads
- Pair of earring wires
- Beading needle #10
- Fireline, 6 lb. test
- **2** pairs of pliers

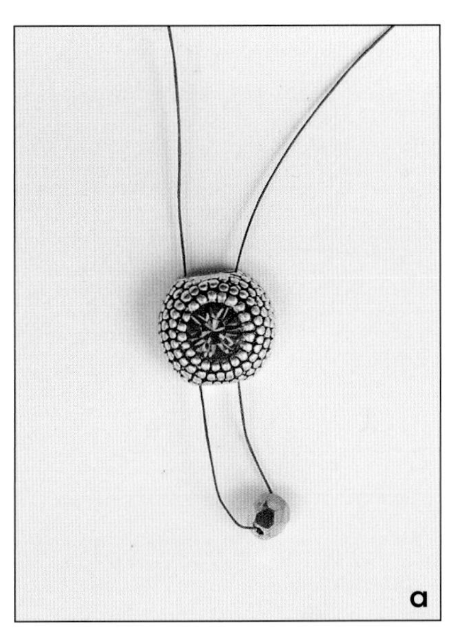
a

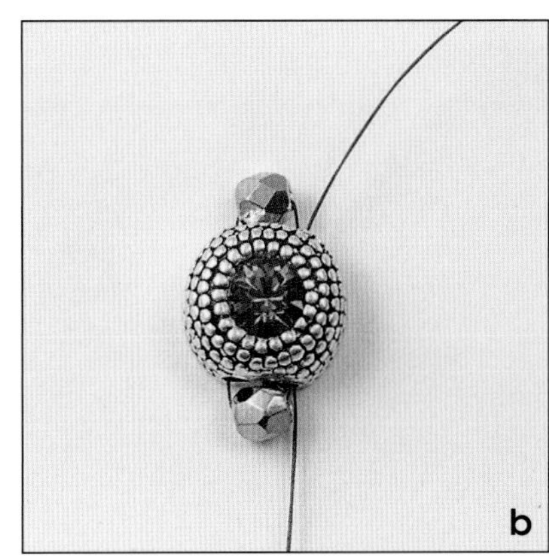
b

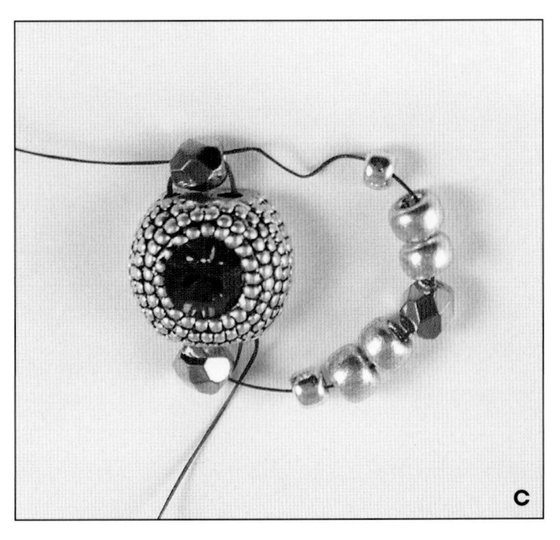
c

d

Earrings

1. Thread a needle on 2 ft. (61cm) of thread. Pick up a slider and a 3mm fire-polished bead, and sew through the available hole of the slider **(photo a)**, leaving an 8-in. (20cm) tail.

2. Pick up a 3mm, and sew back through the first hole of the slider **(photo b)**. Continue through the 3mm added in the previous step.

3. Pick up an $11^{\underline{o}}$ seed bead, two $8^{\underline{o}}$ seed beads, a 3mm, two $8^{\underline{o}}$s, and an $11^{\underline{o}}$, and sew through the 3mm opposite the 3mm your thread exited at the start of this step **(photo c)**. These beads will form a loop around one side of the slider.

4. Work as in step 3 to add a loop of beads around the other side of the slider, and then retrace the thread path through all the beads around the slider to exit the 3mm opposite the tail **(photo d)**.

5. Rotate the beadwork. Pick up an 11º, a 3mm, and an 11º, sew back through the 3mm your thread exited at the start of this step **(photo e)**, and continue through the first 11º and 3mm picked up in this step.

6. Work as in steps 1–4, but at the start of step 2, don't pick up a new 3mm; instead, sew through the 3mm added in step 5 **(photo f)**.

7. Pick up five 11ºs, and sew through the 3mm your thread exited at the start of this step **(photo g)**. Continue through the first two 11ºs picked up in the step, skip the next 11º, and sew through the last two 11ºs and the nearest 3mm. Snug up the beads so the center 11º pops out to form a point **(photo h)**. Sew through the beads around the slider, tying a few half-hitch knots (Basics, p. 12) between the beads. End the working thread (Basics).

8. Thread a needle on the tail and sew through the 3mm at the opposite end of the beadwork from the point created in step 7. Work as in step 7 to create a loop on this end. End the threads **(photo i)**.

9. With roundnose pliers, open the loop of an earring wire (Basics), attach the point at one end of the beadwork, and close the loop.

10. Make a second earring.

Arabesque Earrings

The diamond shape of these earrings with their sharply pointed corners flatters any face shape. Make several in your favorite colorways, then make a few to give away as gifts.

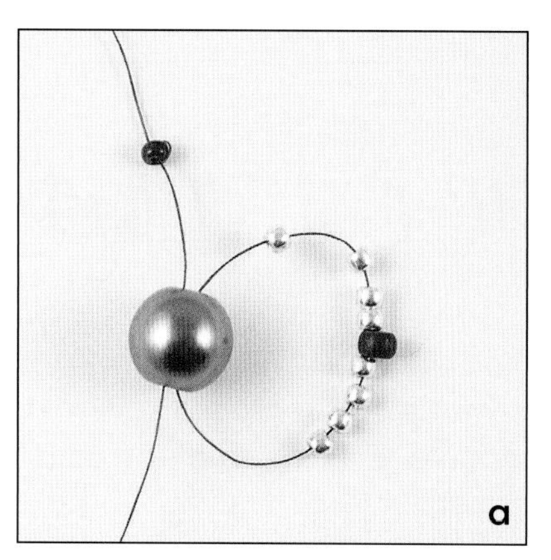
a

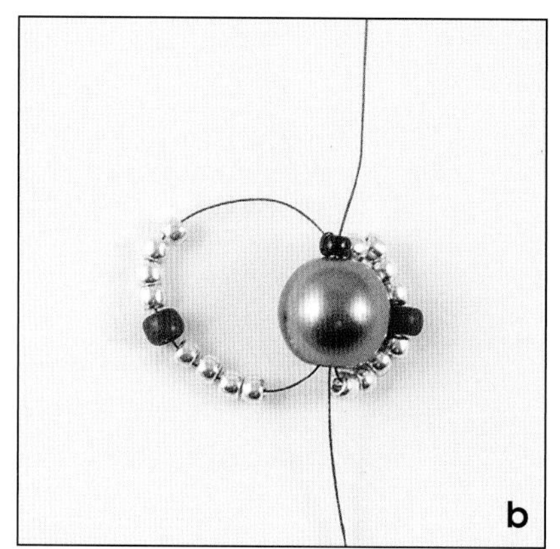
b

c

d

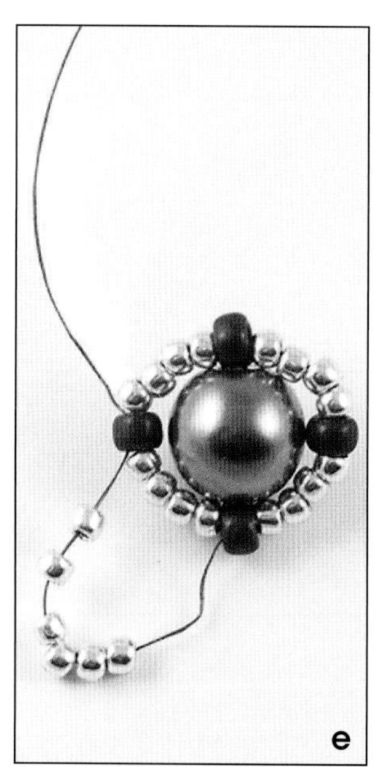
e

f

SUPPLIES

- **2** 8mm glass pearls
- **8** 8º seed beads
- 1g 11º seed beads
- 1g 15º seed beads
- Pair of earring wires
- Beading needle #10
- Fireline, 6 lb. test
- **2** pairs of pliers

Earrings

1. Thread a needle and attach a stop bead (Basics, p. 12) on 2 ft. (61cm) of thread, leaving an 8-in. (20cm) tail. Pick up an 8mm pearl, four 11º seed beads, an 8º seed bead, and four 11ºs, and sew through the pearl again in the same direction so the beads form a half ring around one side of the pearl **(photo a)**.

2. Pick up four 11ºs, an 8º, and four 11ºs, and sew through the pearl again in the same direction. Push these beads to the other side of the pearl **(photo b)**. Sew through the nine beads added in this step, then pick up an 8º and sew through the nine beads added in step 1 **(photo c)**. Pick up an 8º and sew through all 20 beads, forming a ring around the pearl. Exit an 8º **(photo d)**. Remove the stop bead. End the tail (Basics).

3. Pick up six 11ºs, and sew through the next 8º in the original ring **(photo e)**. Repeat this step three times, and then sew through all the beads in this step. Continue through the first six 11ºs picked up in this step **(photo f)**.

4. Pick up three 11ºs, skip the next 8º, and sew through the following six 11ºs **(photo g)**. Repeat this step three times, and step up through the first two 11ºs picked up in this step **(photo h)**.

5. Pick up seven 15º seed beads, and sew back through the 11º your thread exited at the start of this step in the same direction to form a loop **(photo i)**. Retrace the thread path through the loop several times to reinforce and exit the 11º. Continue through the next 18 11ºs.

6. Pick up five 15ºs, and sew through the 11º again **(photo j)**.

7. Skip the first 15º and sew through the following 15º. Snug up the beads so the skipped 15º pops out. Repeat this step once, and then skip the next 15º and sew through the 11º **(photo k)**. Continue through the next 18 11ºs, tying a couple of half-hitch knots between the beads. End the working thread.

8. With roundnose pliers, open the loop of an earring wire (Basics) and attach the loop of beads created in step 5. Close the loop.

9. Make a second earring.

Flying Saucer Earrings

These fun little O-beads add an out-of-this-world element to any design. In these easy earrings, the O-beads orbit around the center pearl like moons around a planet.

SUPPLIES

- **2** 8mm glass pearls
- 1g #1 (3mm) bugle beads
- 1g O-beads
- **20** 11º seed beads
- 1g 15º seed beads
- Pair of earring wires
- Beading needle #10
- Fireline, 6 lb. test

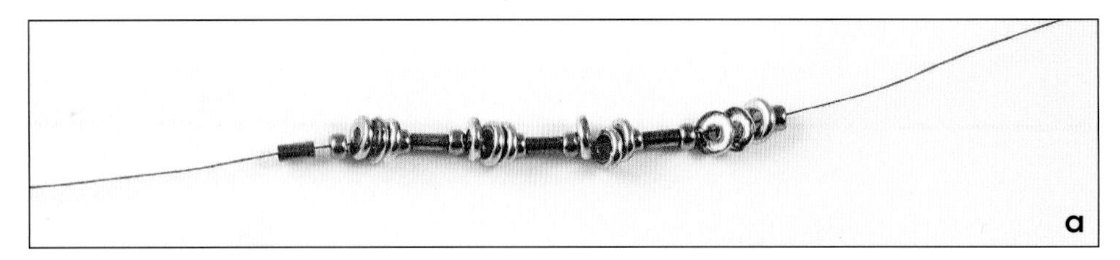
a

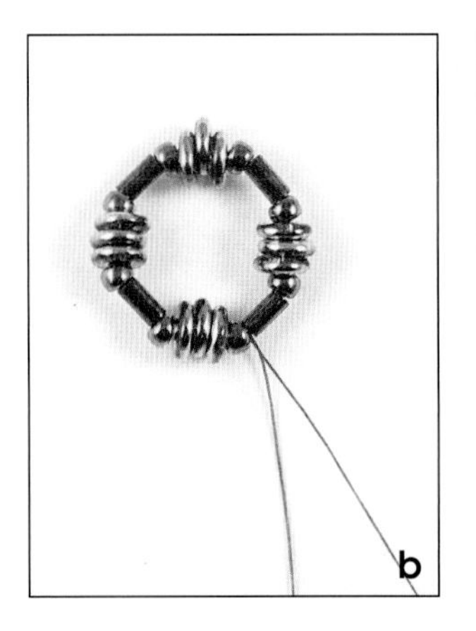
b

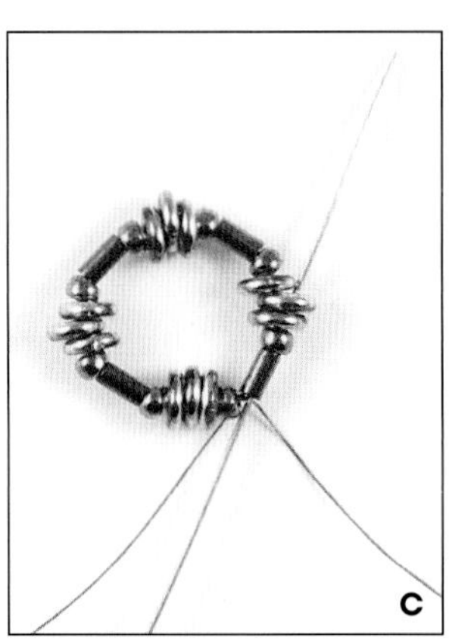
c

Earrings

1. Thread a needle on 2 ft. (61cm) of thread. Pick up a repeating pattern of a 3mm bugle bead, an 11º seed bead, three O-beads, and an 11º for a total of four bugles **(photo a)**. Sew through all the beads again to form a ring **(photo b)**, leaving a 6-in. (15cm) tail. Tie a square knot with the tail (Basics, p. 12).

2. Sew through the beads in the ring to exit a center O-bead in a group of three **(photo c)**. Pick up an 11º, an 8mm glass pearl, and an 11º, and sew through the center O-bead in the group of three on the opposite side of the ring **(photo d)**. Sew back through the 11º, pearl, and 11º added in this step, and continue through the center O-bead **(photo e)**.

d

3. Pick up 10 15º seed beads and the loop of an earring wire. Sew through the second 15º picked up in the opposite direction **(photo f)**. Snug up the beads. Pick up a 15º, and sew through the center O-bead in the opposite direction. Retrace the thread path through the beads in this step.

4. With the thread exiting the center O-bead, sew through all the beads

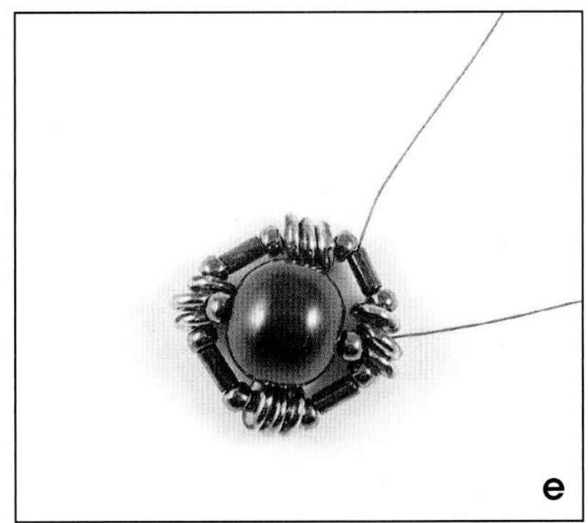

e

around the ring using a firm tension, and tying a couple of half-hitch knots as you go (Basics). End the threads.

5. Make a second earring.

f

Peacock Earrings

I made these earrings specifically to match a necklace I already had. I like them so much, I've lost count as to how many pairs I've made. They remind me a bit of a peacock's tail fanning out—and since I typically use blues, greens, and purples, the name seemed appropriate.

a

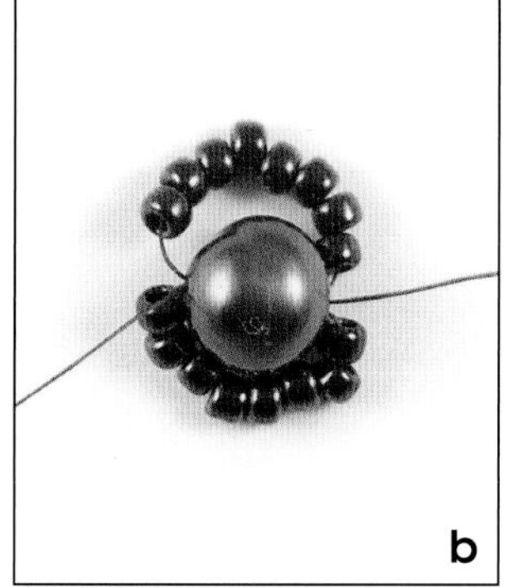

b

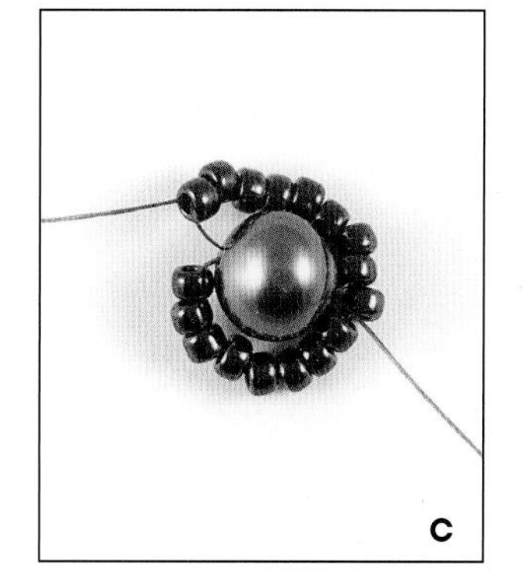

c

SUPPLIES

- **2** 6mm round glass beads or pearls
- 1g 8º seed beads color C (garnet AB)
- 1g 11º seed beads color A (bronze)
- 1g 11º seed beads color B (garnet AB)
- **2** 4mm jump rings
- Pair of earring wires
- Beading needle #10
- Fireline, 6 lb. test
- **2** pairs of chainnose pliers

d

e

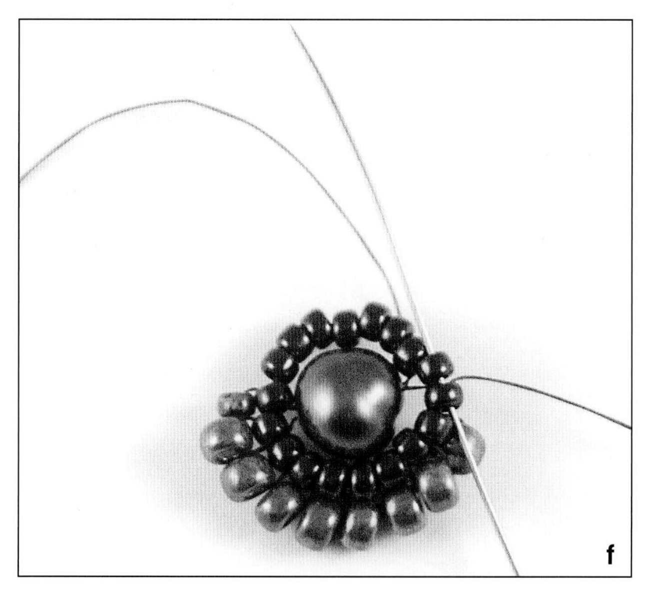

f

Earrings

1. Thread a needle on a comfortable length of thread. Pick up a 6mm round bead and eight color A 11º seed beads. Sew through the pearl in the same direction, leaving a 6-in. (15cm) tail **(photo a)**. The As will form a loop around one half of the 6mm.

2. Pick up eight As, and sew through the pearl again. Push these beads to the other side to form a loop around the other half of the 6mm **(photo b)**.

3. Sew through the eight As added in the previous step, pick up an A, and sew through the eight As picked up in step 1 **(photo c)**. Pick up an A, and sew through all the As around the 6mm.

4. Pick up a color B 11º seed bead and sew through the A directly below in the same direction **(photo d)**. Continue through the next A **(photo e)**.

5. Pick up a color C 8º seed bead, sew through the A your thread exited at the start of this step in the same direction, and continue through the next A. Repeat this step seven times **(photo f)**.

6. Work as in the first part of step 5 using a B **(photo g)**. Sew through the next three As around the 6mm.

7. Pick up seven As and sew back through the A your thread exited at the start of this step in the same direction **(photo h)**. These beads will form a small loop at the top of the earring.

8. Sew through the first A added in the previous step, skip the next A, and sew through the following A **(photo i)**. Snug up the beads so the skipped A pops out **(photo j)**. Skip the next A, sew through the following A, and pull the thread tight to pop out the skipped bead. Repeat this stitch once more **(photo k)**, and then retrace the thread path in this step. End the threads (Basics, p. 12).

9. Open a 4mm jump ring and attach the top seed bead and the loop of an earring wire (Basics). Close the ring.

10. Make a second earring.

Bodacious Bauble Pendant

Creating three-dimensional objects with beads is one of my favorite things, but also one of the most intimidating aspects of learning to bead. The key to successfully stitching this bauble is using a very firm tension and retracing the thread path through the beads. The crystals in the project are large and you need to fill up the holes with thread in order for the pendant to be stable and not wobbly.

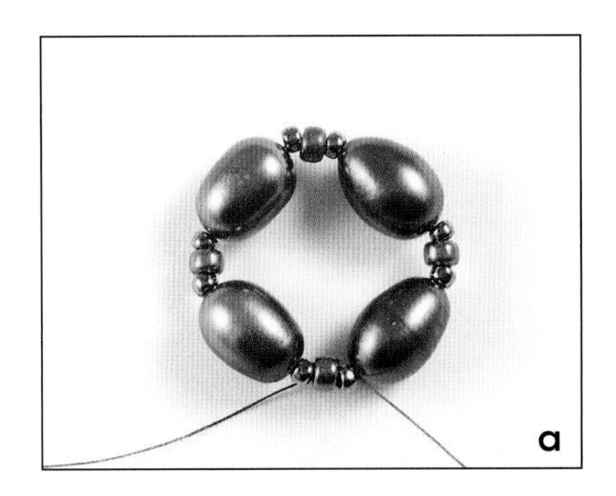
a

b

c

SUPPLIES

- **4** 7x9mm pearls
- **4** 8mm bicone crystals
- **12** 8º seed beads
- 1g 11º seed beads in two colors: A and B
- Beading needle #10
- Fireline, 6 lb. test

d

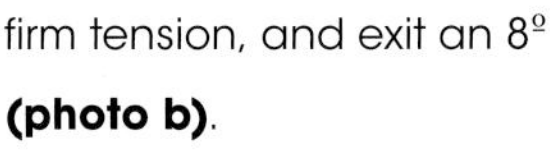

Pendant

1. Thread a needle on 1 yd. (.9m) of thread, and pick up a repeating pattern of a 7x9mm pearl, a color A 11º seed bead, an 8º seed bead, and an A for a total of four pearls. Tie the beads into a ring with a square knot (Basics, p. 12) **(photo a)**, leaving an 8-in. (20cm) tail. Sew through all the beads again, using a firm tension, and exit an 8º **(photo b)**.

2. Pick up an A, an 8º, an A, an 8mm bicone crystal, an A, an 8º, and an A. Sew through the next 8º in the ring **(photo c)**. Repeat this step to complete the round **(photo d)**. Retrace the thread path using a firm tension, pushing the crystals toward the center of the ring. Exit a crystal.

3. Pick up a color B 11º seed bead, and sew through the next crystal **(photo e)**. Repeat this step to complete the round and snug up the beads **(photo f)**. The beadwork will be a little floppy, but do not be concerned. Retrace the thread path two or three times using a firm tension and you will notice the work become firmer. Continue through the beads to exit

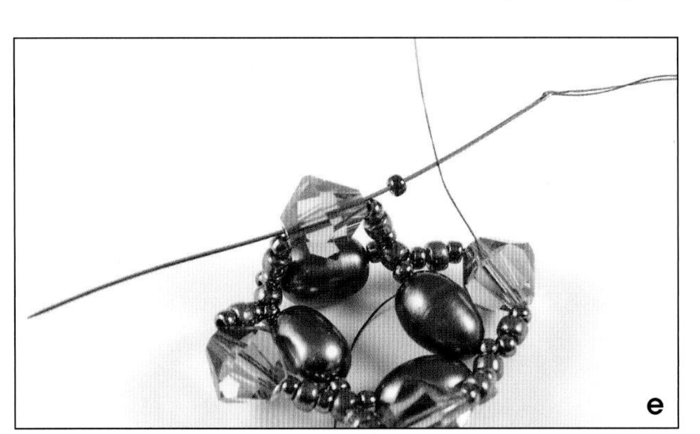
e

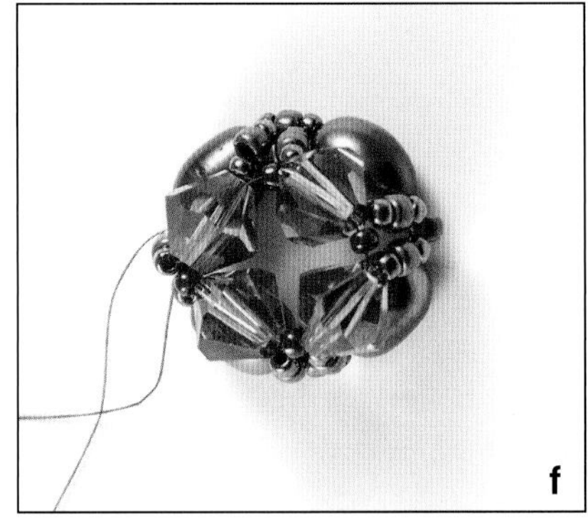
f

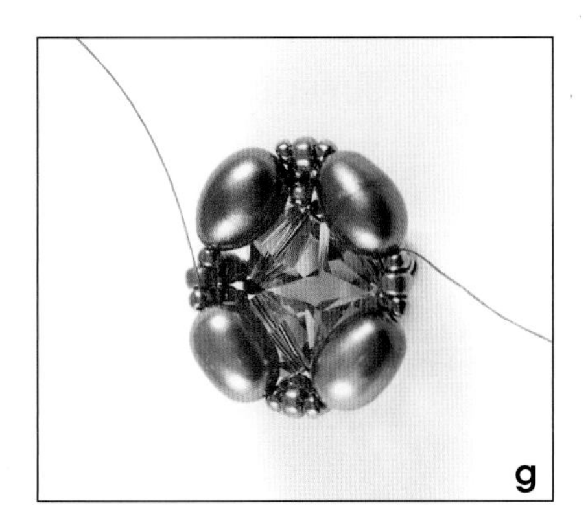

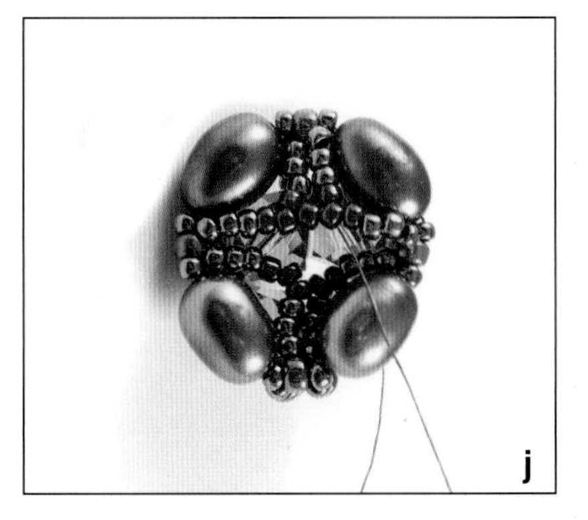

the nearest B, then sew through the adjacent A, 8º, two As, pearl, A, and 8º in the original ring.

4. Turn your beadwork over so the back of the bauble is facing up as in **photo g**. Pick up three As, three Bs, and three As, and sew through the next 8º in the original ring **(photo h)**. Repeat to complete the round using a firm tension, and step up through the first three As and the next two Bs **(photo i)**.

5. Pick up a B and sew through the center B in the next three-B group **(photo j)**. Repeat to complete the round **(photo k)**. Retrace the thread path through the beads in this step several times to secure. End the threads (Basics).

6. To wear, string a ribbon or thin chain under the side bands created in step 2 **(photo l)**.

Designer's Note

To make this bauble really pop, choose a contrasting color for the color B 11º seed beads. Due to their placement in the design, the crystals will pick up the color. I chose a bright metallic for the Bs, and the whole bauble seems to shine with an inner glow.

Chunky Monkey Bracelet

When time is at a premium but you want a substantial piece of jewelry, you have to use bigger beads! Here's a fun, fast, and easy bracelet that works up quickly, but stands out.

tip

I recommend using split rings over jump rings in this project because the larger beads can be quite heavy. Split rings offer a more secure connection than a jump ring, which can be pulled open over time by the weight of the beads.

SUPPLIES

- **32** 6–8mm round glass pearls or gemstone beads
- 2g 8° seed beads
- 1g 11° seed beads
- **2** 6mm split rings
- Toggle clasp
- Beading needle #10
- Fireline, 14 lb. test
- Split ring pliers

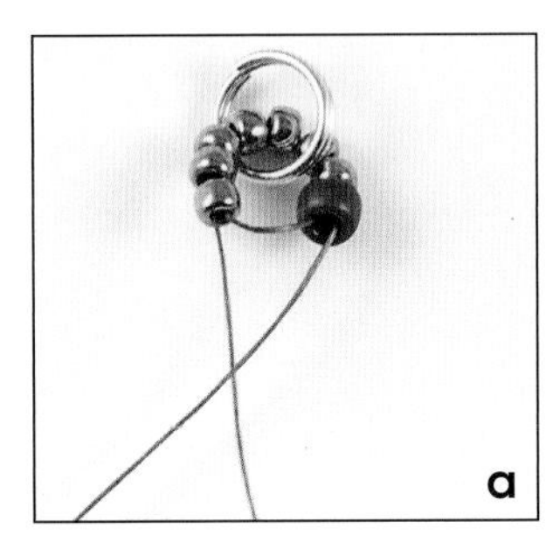
a

b

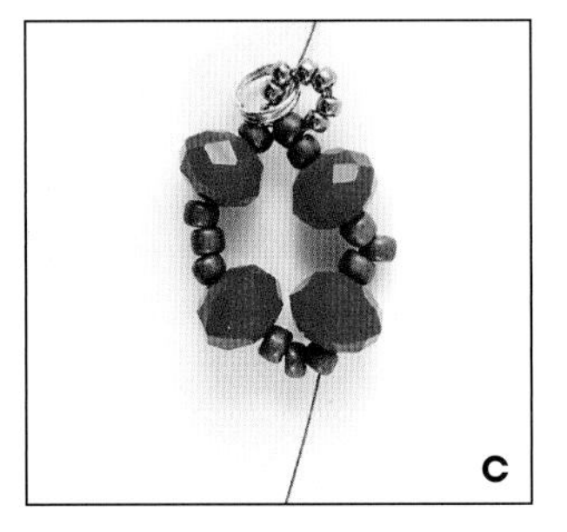
c

d

NOTE For gemstones or other heavy beads, I suggest using 14-lb. test Fireline or doubling your thread.

Bracelet

1. On 1 yd. (.9m) of thread, pick up an 8° seed bead, seven 11° seed beads, and a 6mm split ring, and sew through all the beads and the split ring again to form a ring **(photo a)**, leaving a 6-in. (15cm) tail. Retrace the thread path through the beads and exit the 8°.

2. Pick up an 8°, an 8mm round bead, three 8°s, an 8mm, three 8°s, an 8mm, three 8°s, an 8mm, and an 8°, and sew through the 8° your thread exited at the start of this step **(photo b)**. Step up through the next 8°, 8mm, and 8° in the ring.

3. Skip the next 8°, and sew through the following 8°, 8mm, and 8°. Snug up the beads so the center 8° pops out **(photo c)**. You may need to gently pull it to the outside of the ring with your needle. Repeat this stitch around the ring using a firm tension, and then sew through the beads to exit the center 8° opposite the tail **(photo d)**.

4. Repeat steps 2 and 3 until you have a band the desired length minus 1 in. (2.5cm) for the clasp.

5. Pick up seven 11° s and a 6mm split ring, and sew back through the 8° your thread exited at the start of this step. Sew through all the beads in this loop again several times to reinforce. End the threads (Basics, p. 12).

6. Using split ring pliers, attach one half of the clasp to the split ring at one end of the bracelet (Basics). Repeat for the other half of the clasp and the other end of the bracelet.

Designer's Note

The bigger the beads, the longer the bracelet. For example, I used 32 8mm beads in the orange and bronze bracelet to make a bracelet measuring 8¼ in. (21cm) long. The ruby red bracelet uses 32 6x7mm rondelle beads and measures 7½ in. (19.1cm) long. Armed with this information, you can plan accordingly to make a bracelet to fit your own wrist.

2 HOUR *Projects*

Little Black Dress Ring

Give me two hours (or less) and I'll give you a spectacular pearl ring you made yourself! Pair this cocktail ring with a little black dress for a simply elegant look.

a

b

Ring Top

1. On 1 yd (.9m) of thread, pick up an 8º seed bead, an 8mm glass pearl, an 8º, an 8mm pearl, an 8º, an 8mm pearl, an 8º, and an 8mm pearl, and sew through all the beads again to form a ring **(photo a)**, leaving an 8-in. (20cm) tail. Tie a square knot with the tail (Basics, p. 12). Continue through the next 8º, 8mm pearl, and 8º, and pull on the thread to hide the knot in the beads.

2. Pick up nine 11º seed beads, skip the next 8mm pearl, and sew through the following 8º **(photo b)**. Push this loop of beads along the outer edge of the pearl. Repeat this step three times.

SUPPLIES

- **4** 8mm glass pearls
- **1** 4mm glass pearl
- **4** 8º seed beads
- 1g 11º seed beads
- Beading needles #11 or 12
- Fireline, 6 lb. test

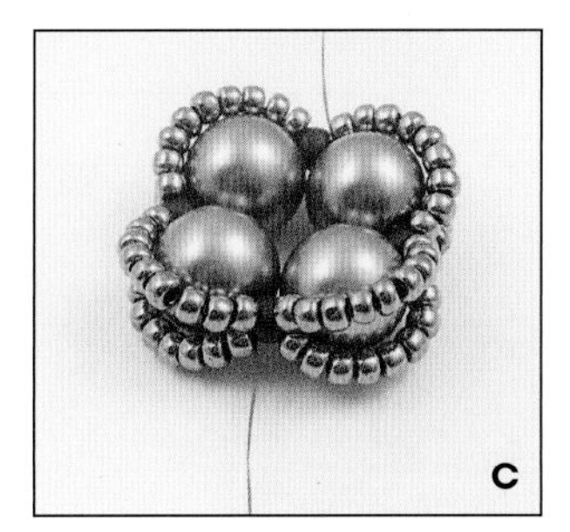
c

3. Work as in step 2 to add a second row of loops to rest above the loops created in the previous step **(photo c)**. Continue through the nearest 8mm pearl.

4. Pick up four 11º seed beads, a 4mm pearl, and four 11ºs, and sew through the 8mm pearl again in the same direction **(photo d)**. The beads you picked up in this step will form a loop. Push the loop to the center of the ring **(photo e)**.

5. Pick up four 11ºs, sew through the 4mm pearl, pick up four 11ºs, and sew through the 8mm pearl again in the same direction to add a second loop above the first loop. Continue through the next 8º, 8mm pearl, 8º, and 8mm pearl in the original ring **(photo f)**.

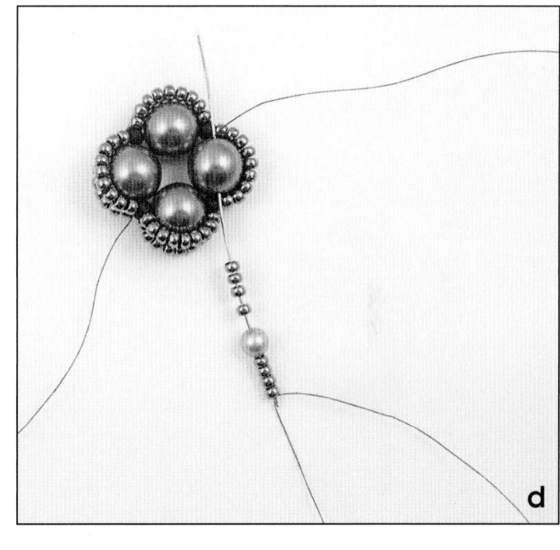
d

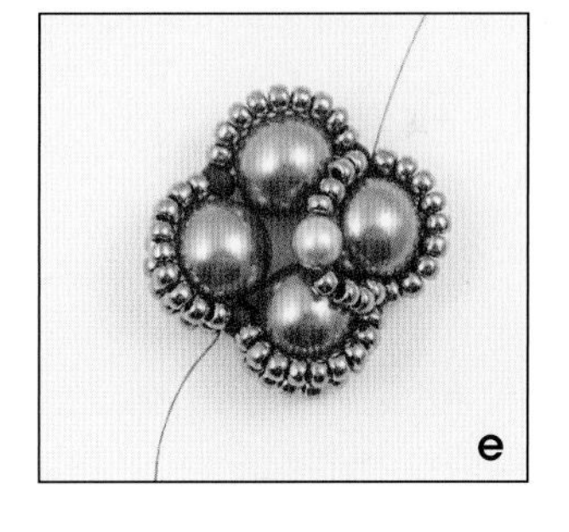
e

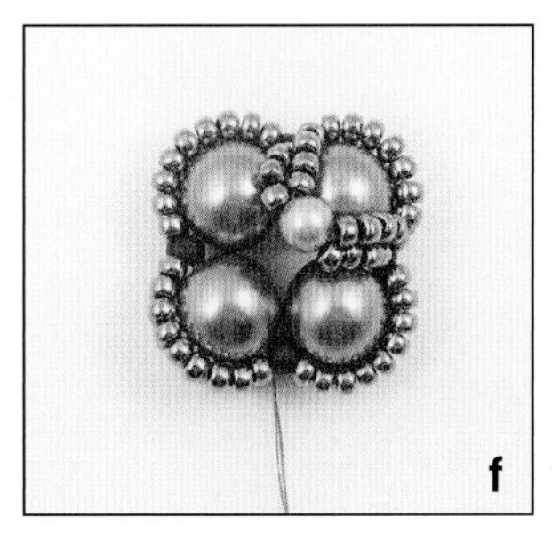
f

g

h

i

j

k

l

6. Pick up four 11ºs, and sew through the 4mm pearl added in step 4. Pick up four 11ºs, and sew through the same 8mm pearl again.

7. Work as in step 6 to add a second loop on this side of the ring top **(photo g)**.

Ring Band

1. Sew through the beadwork to exit the third 11º in a lower nine-bead loop along the outer edge of an 8mm pearl **(photo h)**. Pick up six 11ºs, skip the next three 11ºs in the nine-bead loop, and sew through the remaining three 11ºs in the loop **(photo i)**. Turn, and sew through all nine 11ºs in the upper loop along the outer edge of the same 8mm pearl **(photo j)** with your needle pointing in the opposite direction. Turn, and sew through the first three 11ºs in the lower nine-bead loop again, and continue through the first four 11ºs in the six-bead loop created at the start of this step **(photo k)**.

2. Pick up five 11ºs, and sew back through the third and fourth 11ºs in the six-bead loop created in the previous step **(photo l)**. Continue through the first three 11ºs added in this step **(photo m)**.

3. Pick up seven 11ºs, and sew back through the 11º your thread exited at the start of this step in the same direction **(photo n)**, and continue through the first four 11ºs added in this step. Repeat this step until you have a band that is ¼ in. (6mm) short of fitting around your finger.

4. Thread a needle on the tail, and work as in step 1 to create a six-bead loop opposite the ring band on the other side of the ring top. You may find it easier to work on the back of the ring top **(photo o)**.

5. To join: Pick up two 11ºs, and, making sure the band is not twisted, sew through the center 11º on the end of the ring band. This will be the 11º the working thread is exiting **(photo p)**. Pick up two 11ºs, and sew through the two center 11ºs in the six-bead loop created in the previous step **(photo q)**. End the tail (Basics).

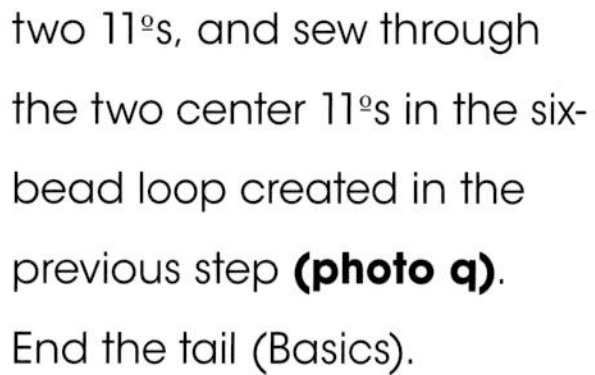

6. With the working thread, retrace the thread path through the join and the length of the band using a firm tension. End the threads.

Designer's Notes

Rings not your thing? Stitch a pendant instead by following all the steps as written for "Ring Top" and then only follow step 1 of "Ring Band." Attach a large (10mm or larger) jump ring to the six-bead loop and string a silk ribbon through the jump ring.

Or make two "Ring Tops," then work as in step 1 of "Ring Band." Attach a 4mm jump ring to each six-bead loop and an earring wire for a classic pair of earrings.

Cupped Rosette Bracelet

I like projects that can be worked on one continuous thread like this bracelet. It seems to come together so quickly and can be completed in a relatively short amount of time. The more rosettes you make, the faster you'll get—so if you're feeling ambitious and have an afternoon, why not make a necklace?

Rosette component

1. On a comfortable length of thread, pick up three 11º seed beads and an 8º seed bead, and sew through all the beads again to form a small ring, leaving a 6-in. (15cm) tail. Tie a square knot (Basics, p. 12) with the tail and retrace the thread path through the ring again to exit the 8º **(photo a)**.

2. Pick up two 11ºs a 4x6mm pearl, an 8º, a pearl, and two 11ºs, and sew through the 8º your thread exited at the start of this step. Continue through all the beads again and step up through the first two 11ºs added in this step **(photo b)**.

SUPPLIES

- **48** 4x6mm glass pearls
- 3g 8º seed beads
- 2g 11º seed beads
- **2** 4mm jump rings
- Toggle clasp
- Beading needle #10
- Fireline, 6 lb. test
- **2** pairs of chainnose pliers

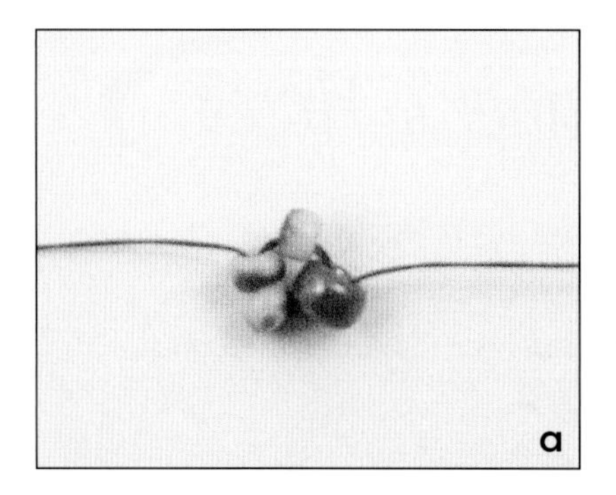
a

b

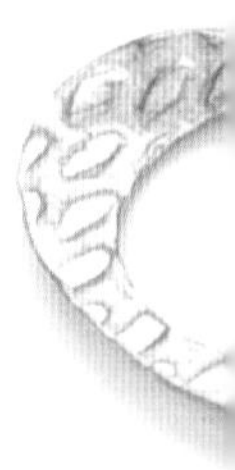

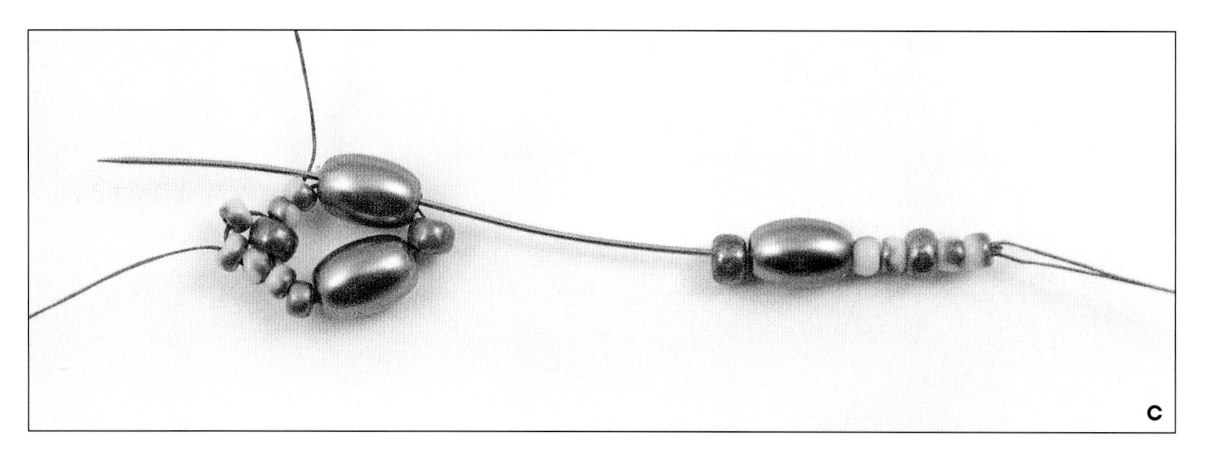

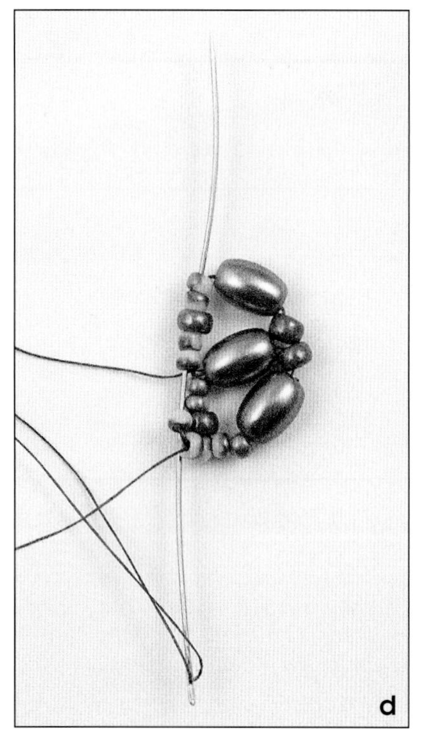

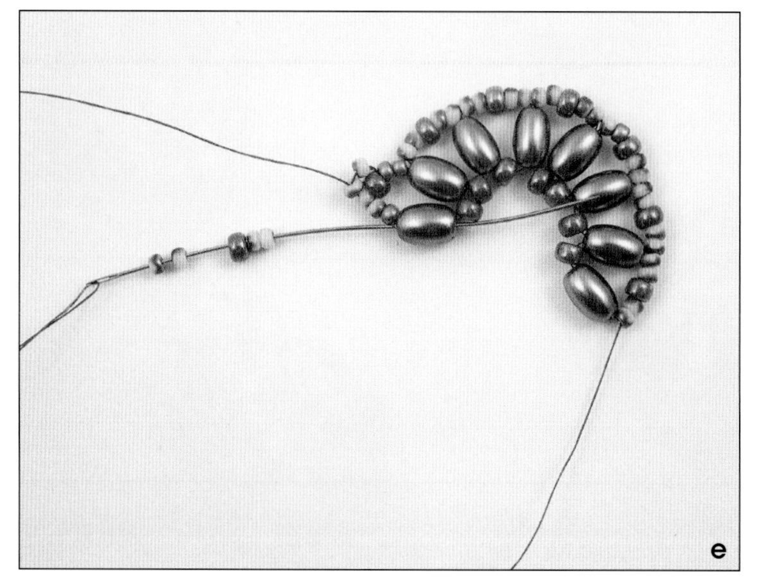

3. Pick up two 11ºs, an 8º, two 11ºs, a pearl, and an 8º, and sew up through the adjacent pearl with the needle pointing toward the tail **(photo c)**. Snug up the beads so the pearls are positioned side by side. Sew through all the beads in this step, and continue through the first five beads picked up in this step **(photo d)**.

4. Work as in step 3 five times, then pick up two 11ºs, an 8º, and two 11ºs, and sew down through the second pearl added in step 2 **(photo e)**. Pick up an 8º, and sew up through the last pearl added in the repeat **(photo f)**. Continue through the two 11ºs, 8º, and two 11ºs along the outside of the ring, and then sew through the nearest pearl and following 8º **(photo g)**.

5. Sew through all eight 8ºs in the center of the ring with a firm tension. Sew through a pearl and then sew

f

g

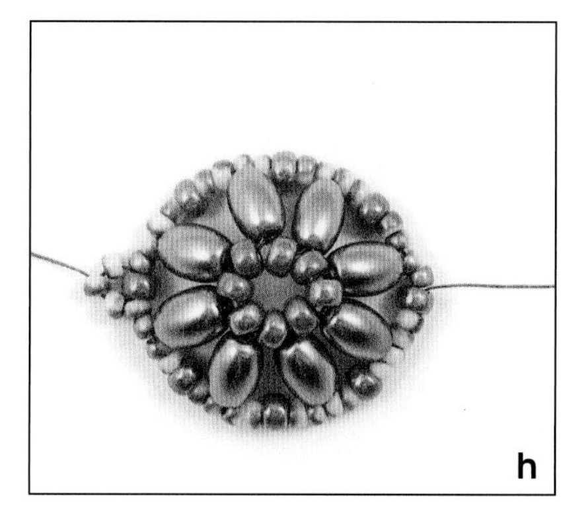
h

i

through all the 11ºs and 8ºs along the outer edge of the ring, using a firm tension. The beadwork will form a domed or cupped rosette. Continue to sew through the beads around the outer edge to exit the 8º opposite the 8º your thread exited in step 1 **(photo h)**.

6. Pick up three 8ºs, and sew through the 8º your thread exited at the start of this step. Continue through the first two 8ºs picked up in this step **(photo i)**.

7. Work as in steps 2–6, ending and adding thread (Basics) as needed until you have a band the desired length, less 1 in. (2.5cm) for the clasp. End the threads (Basics).

8. Open a 4mm jump ring and attach an end loop and one half of the clasp. Close the ring. Repeat for the remaining end of the bracelet and the other half of the clasp.

Darling Dangle Earrings

Over the years I've made more than 500 pairs of earrings—but of all the earrings I've made, this pair has received the most compliments. Maybe it's because they go with everything so I wear them more than any other earrings. Whatever it is, these are my all-time favorites. Even a beginner can make these in less than two hours. An experienced beader can whip these out in under an hour.

SUPPLIES

- **36** 4mm glass pearls
- **4** 4mm bicone crystals
- 2g 11° seed beads
- Pair of earring wires
- Beading needle #10
- Fireline, 6 lb. test

a

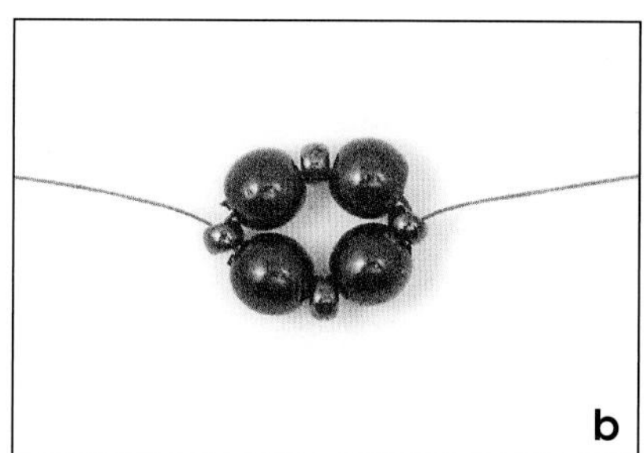

b

c

tip

Going to a party and need a last-minute hostess gift? You will blow her away with these little treasures! I bet the first thing she says is "You MADE these?"

Earrings

1. Thread a needle on 2 ft. (61cm) of thread. Pick up an 11° seed bead, a 4mm pearl, an 11°, a pearl, an 11°, a pearl, an 11° and a pearl, and sew through all the beads again to form a ring **(photo a)**, leaving a 6-in. (15cm) tail. Continue through the next four beads to exit the 11° opposite the tail **(photo b)**.

2. Pick up an 11°, a pearl, and an 11°, and sew through the 11° on the opposite side of the ring **(photo c)**. This will be the 11° the tail is exiting. Then sew back through the 11°, pearl, 11°, and 11° your thread exited at the start of this step, and snug up the beads **(photo d)**. The three beads added in this step will lay across the original ring.

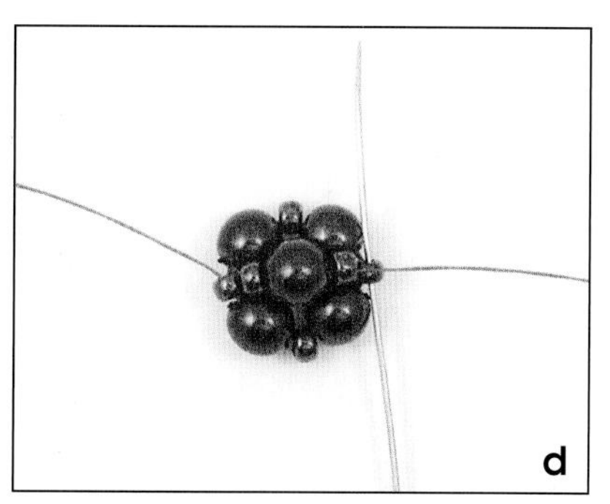

d

e

f

3. Turn the beadwork over and work as in step 2 on the other side of the work to create a two-sided bauble. Your thread should be exiting the 11º in the original ring opposite the tail.

4. To make the connector: Pick up an 11º, a 4mm bicone crystal, and two 11ºs, skip the last 11º just picked up, and sew through the following 11º and bicone crystal **(photo e)**. Pick up an 11º and sew through the 11º your thread exited at the start of this step in the same direction **(photo f)**. Sew through the 11º, bicone crystal, and next two 11ºs to be in position for the next step **(photo g)**.

g

h

i

5. Pick up a 4mm pearl, an 11º, a pearl, an 11º, a pearl, an 11º and a pearl and sew through the 11º you exited at the start of this step to form a ring. Retrace the thread path through the beads in this step. Work as in steps 1–3 to create another bauble after the connector, making sure the new bauble is snugged up against the connector **(photo h)**.

6. Work as in step 4 to make a second connector, and then work as in step 5 to make a third bauble. Sew through the beadwork, tying occasional half-hitch knots (Basics, p. 12). End the working thread (Basics).

7. Thread a needle on the tail, pick up five 11ºs and the loop of an earring wire, and sew through the 11º in the original ring **(photo i)**. Retrace the thread path several times to secure, tying a couple of half-hitch knots. End the thread.

7. Make a second earring.

Light the Lantern Pendant

The latticework of beads allows the light to shine through in this Moroccan-inspired pendant. Stitch with a firm tension to encase a fancy stone in a web of beadwork you can string on a chain, leather cord, or silk ribbon.

SUPPLIES

- **1** 18x25mm fancy stone crystal
- 1g 8º seed beads
- 1g 11º seed beads in **2** colors: A and B
- 1g 15º seed beads
- **2** 4mm jump rings
- Beading needle #10
- Fireline, 6 lb. test
- **2** pairs of pliers

a

b

c

d

Pendant

1. Thread a needle on 1 yd. (.9m) of thread. Pick up 32 8º seed beads and sew through all the beads again to form a ring. Tie a square knot with the tail (Basics, p. 12), leaving a 6-in. (15cm) tail **(photo a)**. Sew through all the beads again and continue through the first two 8ºs.

2. Pick up three 8ºs, skip the next 8º in the original ring, and sew through the following nine 8ºs **(photo b)**. This forms your first corner and these nine beads form the long side of the bezel. Pick up three 8ºs, skip the next 8º, and sew through the following five 8ºs **(photo c)**. This will be a short side and forms another corner. Repeat this step once to form the corners and identify the remaining long and short sides of the bezel. Step up through the first two 8ºs picked up in this step **(photo d)**. Your thread is exiting the center bead in a corner.

3. Place your fancy stone on top of the beadwork, matching long and short sides. The corners will just be visible as shown in **photo e**. This is just to give you an idea of how we are going to construct this bezel. Remove the stone.

4. Pick up an 8º, six color A 11º seed beads, an 8º, six As, and an 8º, and sew through the center 8º in the next corner **(photo f)**.

5. Pick up an 8º, three As, an 8º, three As, and an 8º, and sew through the center 8º in the next corner.

6. Work as in steps 4 and 5 to complete the round. Step up through the first 8º picked up in step 4. Place the stone in the bezel.

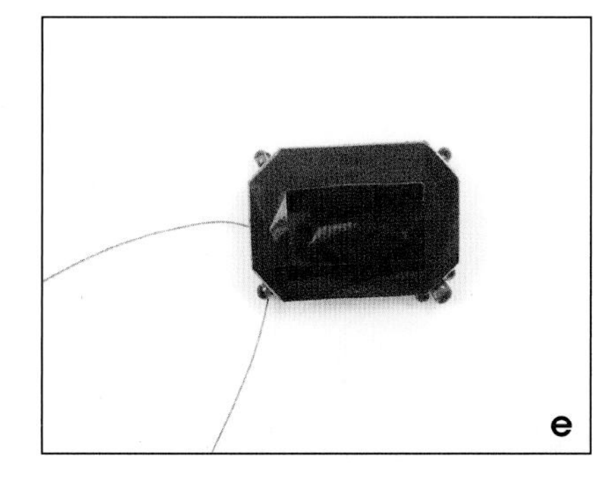

e

f

7. First corner: Pick up a color B 11º seed bead and sew through the third 8º in the previous round, skip the center 8º in this corner, and continue through the 8º your thread exited at the start of this step **(photo g)**. Retrace the thread path and snug up the beads. Continue through the next beads along the long edge of the bezel to exit the third 8º in the next corner **(photo h)**.

g

h

8. Second corner: Pick up a B and sew through the third 8º in the previous round, skip the center 8º in this corner, and sew through the 8º your thread exited at the start of this step. Retrace the thread path and snug up the beads. Continue through the beads along the short edge of the bezel to exit the third 8º in the corner.

9. Third corner: Work as in step 7.

10. Fourth corner: Work as in step 8 **(photo i)**.

i

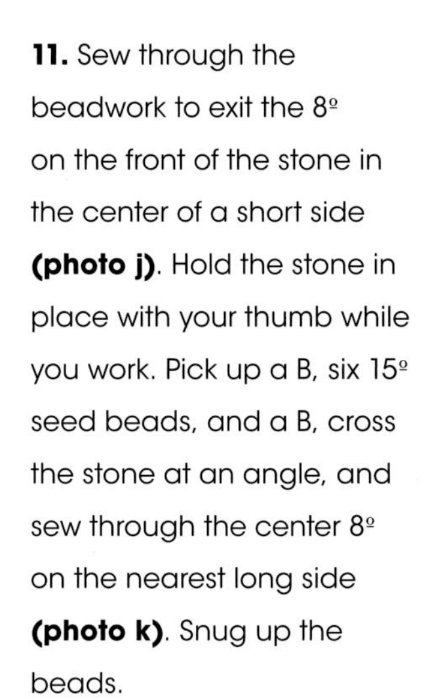

11. Sew through the beadwork to exit the 8º on the front of the stone in the center of a short side **(photo j)**. Hold the stone in place with your thumb while you work. Pick up a B, six 15º seed beads, and a B, cross the stone at an angle, and sew through the center 8º on the nearest long side **(photo k)**. Snug up the beads.

j

k

l

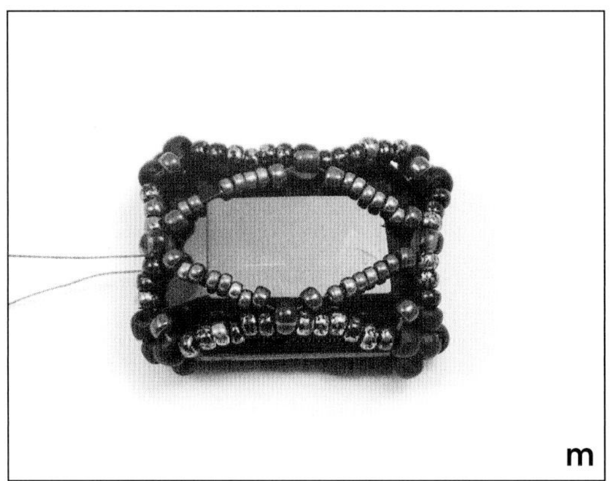
m

n

o

Pick up a B, six 15ºs, and a B, and sew through the center 8º on the remaining short side **(photo l)**.

12. Using a firm tension, work as in step 11 to add the lattice beadwork to the other side of the stone **(photo m)**.

13. At this point, the stone may still slide around in the beadwork. To stabilize the stone, sew through the beadwork to exit an A at the corner on a long side as shown in **photo n**. Pick up three As, skip three 8ºs in the original ring on the back of the stone, and sew through the center three 8ºs **(photo o)**. Pick up three As and sew through the first A before the 8ºs at the corner on the front of the stone **(photo p)**. Continue through the next 8º and the beads in the short side on the front of the stone, tying a couple of half-hitch knots between the beads (Basics) to keep the tension. Exit the first A after the 8º along the other long side.

14. Work as in step 13 to secure the stone on this side of the bezel, then sew through the beadwork to

p

exit the 8º on the front of the stone in the center of the nearest short side **(photo q)**.

15. Pick up five As, an 8º, and five As, and sew through the center 8º in the corresponding short side on the back of the stone. Pick up five As, sew through the 8º just picked up, pick up five 8ºs, and sew through the 8º your thread exited at the start of this step in the same direction to create a loop to string the pendant. Retrace the thread path and end the working thread (Basics).

16. Thread a needle on the tail, and sew through the beadwork to the short side opposite the loop created in the previous step, and exit the center 8º in the original ring on the back of the stone. Pick up three As, and sew through the nearest center 8º in the short side on the front of the stone. Pick up an A, sew through the second A picked up in this step, pick up an A, and sew through the 8º your thread exited at the start of this step **(photo r)**. Retrace the thread path and end the threads (Basics).

q

r

Some people are allergic to the foil on the back of these stones. If you aren't sure or you're making this as a gift and don't know if the recipient is allergic to the foil, it's best to take precautions. You can place two rows of beads at the highest point on the back of the stone to protect the wearer.

Do not end the working thread in step 15; instead, sew through the beadwork to exit the center 8º on a long side on the back of the beadwork. Pick up eight As and sew through the corresponding 8º in the opposite long side. Snug up the beads. Pick up eight As and sew through the 8º your thread exited at the start of this step **(photo s)**. Retrace the thread path through the beads in this step several times, using a firm tension and tying a couple of half-hitch knots between the beads. End the working thread.

s

Omm Ombré Bangle

The bangle is not only meditative to stitch, but comfortable to wear. You can't go wrong with the colors you choose. Try a subtle palette or vibrant, contrasting tones to customize a bracelet that's so quick to stich up, you can make one to match any mood!

Bangle

1. Thread a needle on a comfortable length of thread. Pick up six color A 8º seed beads and tie the beads into a ring with a square knot (Basics, p. 12), leaving a 6-in. (15cm) tail **(photo a)**.

2. Stitch as follows, ending and adding thread (Basics) as needed:

Round 1: Work a round of tubular herringbone: Sew up through the first A **(photo b)**, pick up two As, and sew down through the next A **(photo c)**. Repeat this stitch two times, and step up through the first A added in this round to be in position for the next round **(photo d)**. Your beadwork will begin to form a tube.

Rounds 2 and 3: Work two rounds using color B 8º seed beads.

Rounds 4 and 5: Work two rounds using color C 8º seed beads.

SUPPLIES

- 3g 8° seed beads in each of five colors: A, B, C, D, E
- 7–8 in. (18–20cm) 3mm leather cord
- **2** 3mm crimps
- **2** 4mm jump rings
- **2** split rings
- Beading needle #10
- Fireline, 6 lb. test
- **2** pairs of chainnose pliers
- Split ring pliers

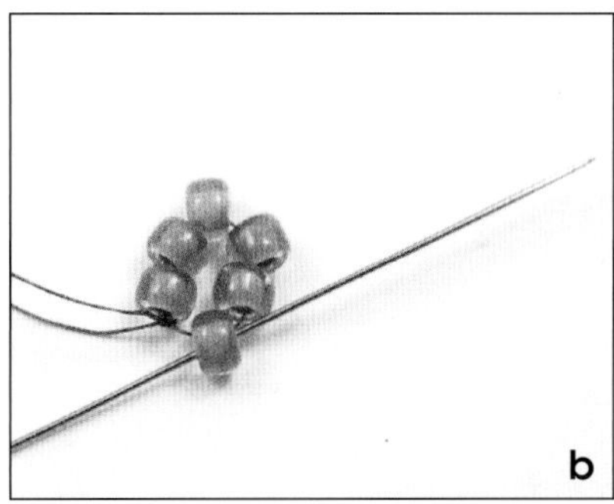

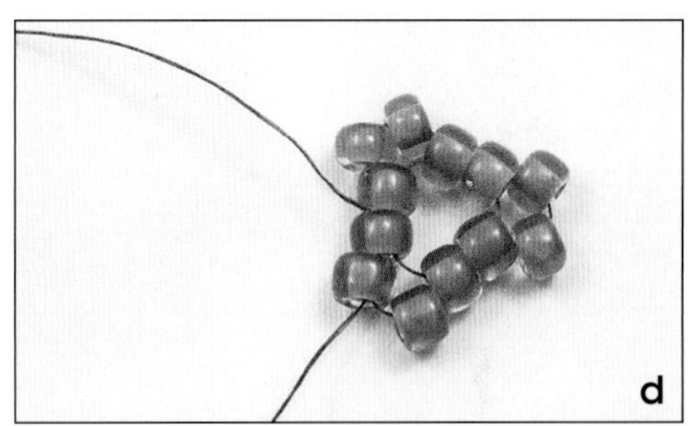

Rounds 6 and 7: Work two rounds using color D 8° seed beads.

Rounds 8–15: Work eight rounds using color E 8° seed beads.

Rounds 16 and 17: Work two rounds using Ds.

Rounds 18 and 19: Work two rounds using Cs.

Rounds 20 and 21: Work two rounds using Bs.

Rounds 22–25: Work four rounds using As.

Rounds 26 and 27: Work two rounds using Bs.

Rounds 28 and 29: Work two rounds using Cs.

Rounds 30 and 31: Work two rounds using Ds.

Rounds 32–39: Work eight rounds using Es.

Rounds 40 and 41: Work two rounds using Ds.

Rounds 42 and 43: Work two rounds using Cs.

Rounds 44 and 45: Work two rounds using Bs.

Rounds 46–49: Work four rounds using As.

Rounds 50 and 51: Work two rounds using Bs.

Rounds 52 and 53: Work two rounds using Cs.

Rounds 54 and 55: Work two rounds using Ds.

Rounds 56–61: Work six rounds using Es.

Rounds 62 and 63: Work two rounds using Ds.

Rounds 64 and 65: Work two rounds using Cs.

Rounds 66 and 67: Work two rounds using Bs.

Rounds 68 and 69: Work two rounds using As, and end the threads.

3. Using chainnose pliers, crimp a crimp end on one end of the 3mm leather cord **(photo e)**. Insert the available end of the cord into the herringbone tube. Trim the end of the cord and attach a crimp end to this end.

4. Using split ring pliers, attach a 4mm split ring (Basics) to a crimp and one

half of the clasp **(photo f)**. Repeat on the remaining end of the bracelet.

Raw Power Hoop Earrings

These are the perfect earrings to go with your power suit. Sparkly and bold, they make a strong statement and will not be ignored. If you're comfortable with cubic right-angle weave (CRAW), you'll be able to make a pair of these in under an hour. If this stitch is new to you, take your time to learn it here. Once you "see" it, you'll love it.

SUPPLIES

- **28** 3mm fire-polished beads or bicone crystals
- **16** 8º seed beads
- 1g 11º seed beads
- 1g 15º seed beads
- Pair of earring wires
- Beading needle #10
- Fireline, 6 lb. test

tip

Cubic right-angle weave (CRAW) can be somewhat difficult to master, but I think the answer lies in thinking of it in terms of an apartment building and the ability to "see" the four-bead units that make up the four "walls," the "ceiling" (top), and "floor" (bottom) of the cube. Once you understand how the cube is constructed, you'll have no trouble mastering this architectural stitch.

CRAW Tube

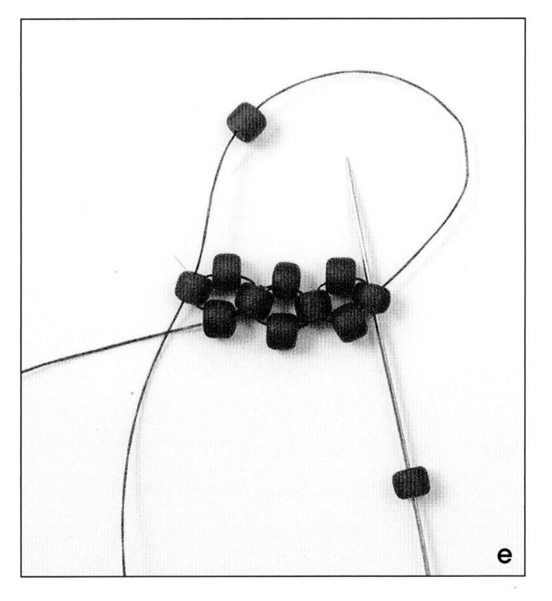

1. Thread a needle on 1 yd. (.9m) of thread. Pick up four 11º seed beads and tie the beads into a ring with a square knot (Basics, p. 12), leaving an 8-in. (20cm) tail. Sew through the beads again and continue through the first two 11ºs again **(photo a)**. This completes the first right-angle weave stitch.

2. Pick up three 11ºs, and sew through the 11º your thread exited at the start of this step. Continue through the first two 11ºs picked up in this step **(photo b)**. Repeat this step once more **(photo c)**.

3. Join to make a cube: Pick up an 11º, sew through the end 11º in the first right-angle weave stitch **(photo d)**, pick up an 11º, and sew through the 11º your thread exited at the start of this step. **Photo e** shows your work before you snug up the beads. **Photo f** shows your work after you pull the beads close together. Take note of the four beads that form the top of the unit. Sew through these four beads using a firm tension to stabilize your work. This completes one CRAW unit.

4. Subsequent units build off of the top of the previous unit. Think of it in terms of the "ceiling" of the previous unit becoming the "floor" of the next unit—much like a high-rise building. With the thread exiting one of the four beads in the "ceiling" of the previous unit, pick up three 11ºs and sew through the 11º your thread is exiting to form a four-bead "wall" **(photo g)**. Continue through the first 11º picked up in this step to be in position to form the adjacent wall. Remember that the "ceiling" of the previous unit is now the "floor" of the current unit.

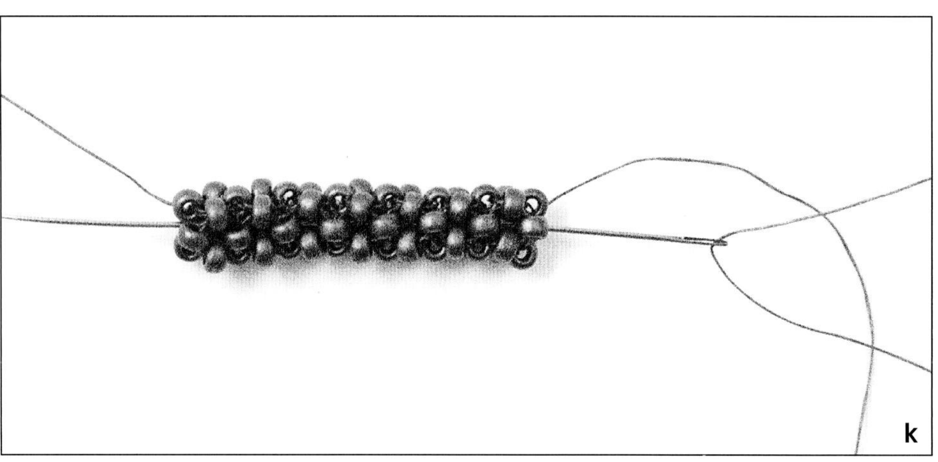

5. Pick up two 11ºs, and sew through the next "floor" 11º and the 11º your thread exited at the start of this step **(photo h)**. Continue through the first two beads picked up in this step and the next floor bead.

6. Pick up two 11ºs, sew down through the nearest 11º added in the previous step **(photo i)**, and continue through the next floor bead, which is also the bead your thread exited at the start of this step. Continue through the first 11º picked up in this step.

7. This is the joining unit and you're only going to add the "ceiling" bead and connect the walls and floor beads: Pick up an 11º, and sew down through the nearest 11º "wall" bead in the first wall created in step 4. Continue through the nearest floor bead, the 11º your thread exited at the start of this step, and the ceiling bead just added in this step. Notice the four beads that form the ceiling of this CRAW. Sew through those four beads with a firm tension **(photo j)**. This completes the second CRAW unit.

8. Work as in steps 4–7 five more times for a total of seven CRAW units.

Assembly

1. Sew through the center of the CRAW tube **(photo k)** to exit the same end as the tail. Pick up a repeating pattern of a 3mm bicone crystal, a 15º seed bead, an 11º, and a 15º four times, then pick up a 15º and the loop of an earring wire to complete the first half of the hoop. Work as in the previous stitch to make a mirror image for the second half of the hoop **(photo l)**. Sew through the center of the CRAW tube in the same

direction and continue through all of the beads in this step and snug up the beads **(photo m)**.

2. Retrace the thread path several times, but on the last pass through the beads, snug up the beads so the 3mm at each end of the tube fits snugly into the end and the tube curves slightly. Tie a couple of half-hitch knots (Basics) between the beads.

Embellishment

1. Sew through the beadwork to exit an 11º at the nearest end of the CRAW tube **(photo n)**. Pick up a 15º and sew through the next 11º along the inner edge **(photo o)**. Repeat this stitch, adding a 15º between each 11º. Gently snug up the beads so the tube curves slightly.

2. At the end of the row, sew through the adjacent 11º **(photo p)**, pick up a 15º, and sew through the next 11º along this inner edge of the tube **(photo q)**. Repeat this stitch, working your way back towards the opposite end of the tube. You now have two rows of 15ºs between the 11ºs and this forces the tube to curve along one side. If necessary, twist the tube to make sure the curve is toward the inside of the hoop.

3. Notice which way the earring wire is facing so you can determine which side is the front of the tube **(photo r)**. Working along the available edge on the front of the tube, pick up an 11º and sew through the next 11º along the lower front edge of the tube. Pick up a 3mm, and sew through the next 11º in the row. Repeat this stitch until you have sewn through the last 11º in the column. Pick up an 11º and sew through the adjacent 11º at the end of the tube toward the last remaining edge.

4. Working on the back of the tube, pick up an 11º seed bead, and sew through the next 11º along the edge. Work the next six stitches in this manner, using 8º seed beads between each 11º. At the end of the row, pick up an 11º, and sew through the four 11ºs around the end of the tube **(photo s)**. End the threads (Basics).

5. Make a second earring.

Designer's Notes

If you like larger earrings, simply increase the length of the CRAW tube. The alabaster pair shown here are based on a 10 CRAW unit tube. These earrings would make a perfect gift for a bride.

For earrings with a more circular shape, work as directed above, but in "Assembly," insert a 3-in. (7.6cm) length of beading wire through the center of the tube, string the repeating pattern on each end, and then slide each end through a crimp bead. Snug up the beads and crimp the crimp. Trim the ends of the wire close to the crimp. Using two pairs of pliers, open the loop of an earring wire, and attach the hoop of the earring. Close the loop. Embellish as directed above. The beading wire provides more support than the thread, and the end result is an earring that is more circular than teardrop shaped.

Last Dance Choker

The last dance is the one you always remember. This delicate necklace is no less powerful. Imagine wearing this little beauty with a sweetheart neckline, the crystals twinkling in the spotlight. Not overpowering—just quietly elegant and memorable.

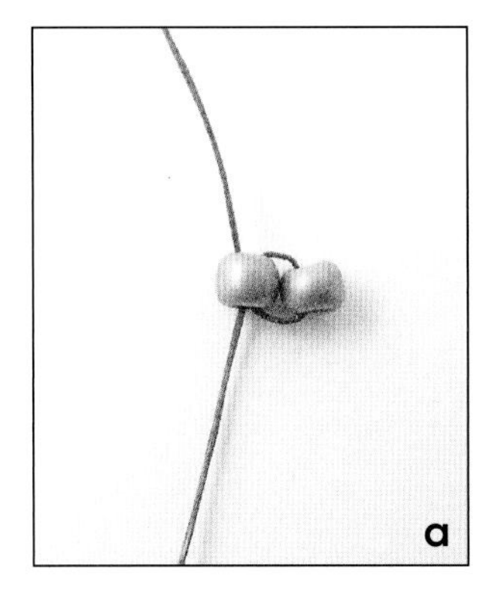

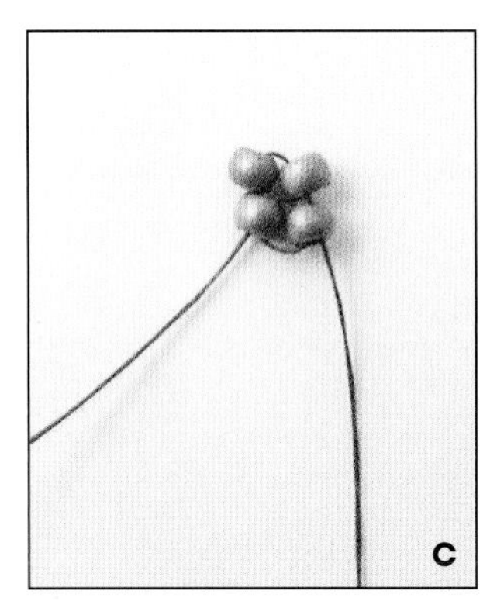

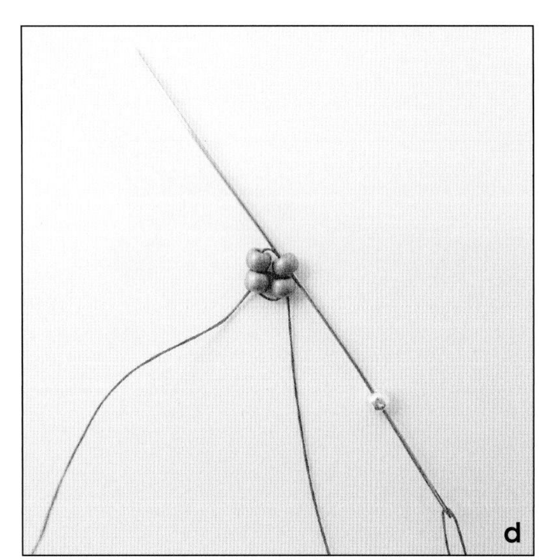

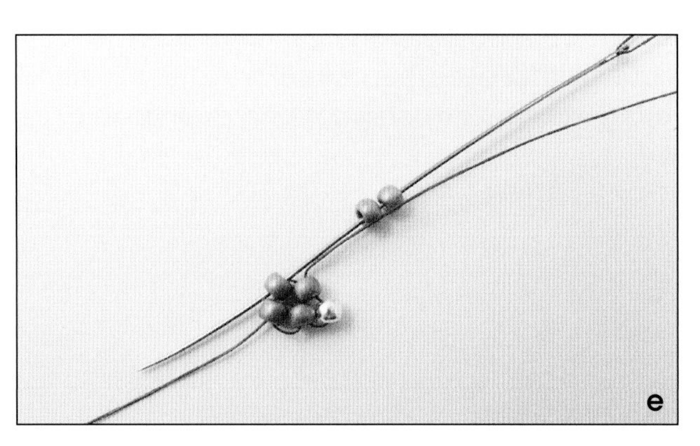

Flat Herringbone Band

1. Thread a needle on a comfortable length of thread. Pick up two color A 11º seed beads and sew through the first A again in the same direction, leaving an 8-in. (20cm) tail. The two As will line up side by side **(photo a)**.

2. Pick up two As and sew down through the second A added in the previous step **(photo b)**. The two new As will sit on top of the two beads in the previous row to form two columns of beads **(photo c)**.

3. Pick up a color B 11º seed bead, and sew up through the A directly above the A your thread exited at the start of this step **(photo d)**.

4. Pick up two As, and sew down through the A opposite the A your thread exited at the start of this step **(photo e)**.

5. Work as in steps 3 and 4 until you have a band measuring 15½ in. (39.4cm) long or the desired length, ending and adding thread (Basics, p. 12) as needed.

6. Pick up five As and sew down through the A opposite the A your thread is exiting to form a loop **(photo f)**. Sew up through the adjacent A and retrace the thread path through the beads in this step several times.

Embellishment Top Edge

1. Sew through the beadwork to exit the end B along one edge with your needle pointing toward the opposite end of the band **(photo g)**. Pick up an A, and sew through the next B along this edge **(photo h)**.

2. Continue to work as in step 1, adding an A between each B along this edge.

3. After you've sewn through the last B along this edge, sew through the beadwork to exit the first A in the nearest column **(photo i)**, and snug up the beads just slightly so the band forms a gentle curve. Tie a half-hitch knot between the beads (Basics) to keep the tension and graceful shape.

4. Pick up five As and sew down through the A your thread exited at the start of this step to form a loop on this end of the band. Retrace the thread path several times, tying a couple of half-hitch knots between the beads. End the threads.

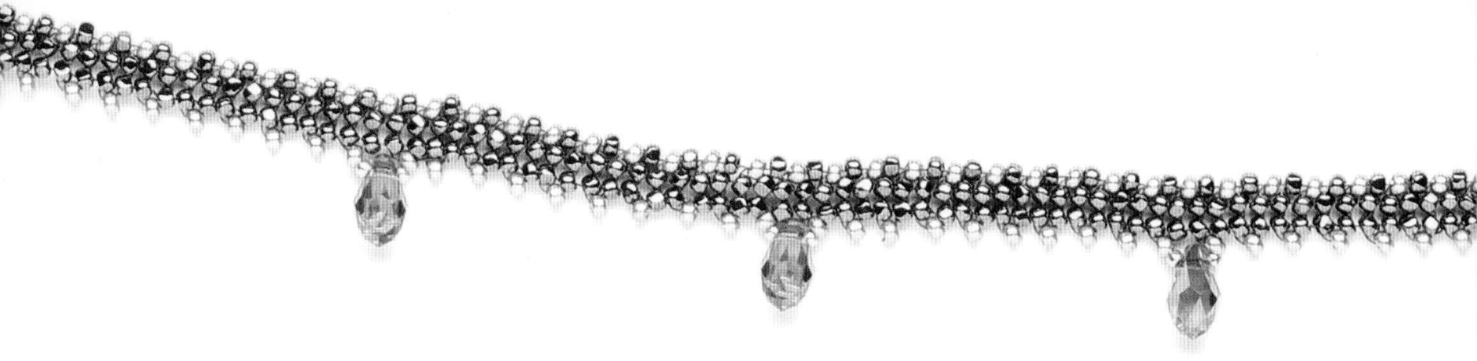

f

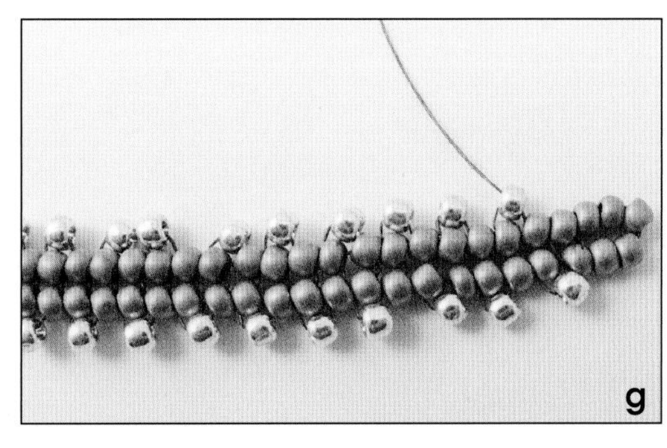
g

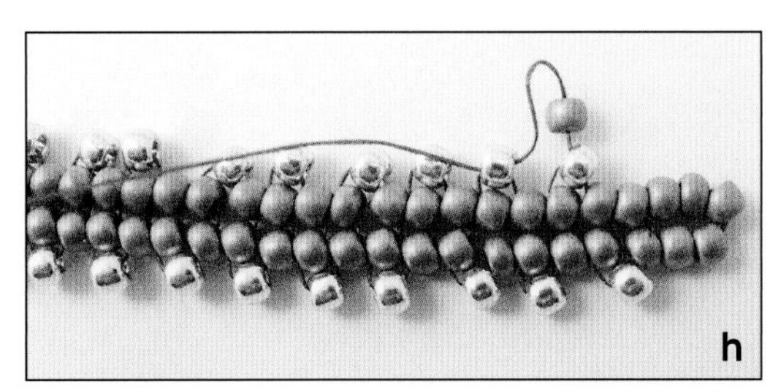
h

SUPPLIES

- **6** 10x6mm crystal or glass drop beads
- 5–6g 11º seed beads color A
- 2g 11º seed beads color B
- **2** 4mm jump rings
- Toggle clasp
- Beading needle #10
- Fireline, 6 lb. test
- **2** pairs of chainnose pliers

i

j

Embellishment Lower Edge

1. Locate the center of the band and add 2 ft. (61cm) of thread. Sew through the beadwork to exit a B along the lower edge approximately ¾ in. (1.9cm) to one side of the center. Working out from the center of the band, pick up two Bs, a 10x6mm drop, and two Bs, and sew through the next B, and adjacent A in the lower column **(photo j)**.

2. Work as in step 1 to add a drop embellishment every 1½ in. (3.8cm), working first toward one end. For my band, I added four drops between the center and one end of the band. I ended the thread, started a new thread near the center again, and worked my way out toward the other end of the band. If your band is longer than 15½ in. (39.4cm), increase the distance between drops; just make sure they are evenly spaced along the band as measured out from the center. End all threads.

Clasp

1. Open a 4mm jump ring and attach the bead loop at one end of the band and the loop of one half of the clasp (Basics). Close the ring.

2. Repeat step 1 on the other end of the band with the other half of the clasp.

3 HOUR *Projects*

Flying Saucer Bracelet

Similar to the Flying Saucer Earrings on p. 26, this project uses those little **UFO-beads**. In this bracelet, you'll not only learn a technique for creating connecting units to join components together, but you'll practice embellishing the connecting units in a way that provides more stability to your beadwork.

SUPPLIES

- **5 or 6** 8mm glass pearls
- 2g #1 (3mm) bugle beads
- **24** 3mm fire-polished beads
- 2g 3mm magatamas
- 2g O-beads
- **6** 8º seed beads
- 2g 11º seed beads
- 1g 15º seed beads
- Toggle clasp
- Beading needle #10
- Fireline, 6 lb. test

Saucer Component

1. Thread a needle on a comfortable length of thread. Pick up a repeating pattern of a 3mm bugle bead, an 11º seed bead, three O-beads, and an 11º for a total of four bugles. Sew through all the beads again to form a ring, and tie a square knot (Basics, p. 12), leaving an 8-in. (20cm) tail.

2. Sew through the beads to exit an 11º before a bugle **(photo a)**. Pick up a bugle, skip the bugle in the previous round, and sew through the next five beads **(photo b)**. This bugle will sit on top of the bugle added in step 1. Repeat this step to complete the round.

3. Sew through the beads in the ring to exit a center O-bead in a group of three **(photo c)**. Pick up an 11º, an 8mm glass pearl, and an 11º, and sew through the center O-bead in the group of three on the opposite

a

b

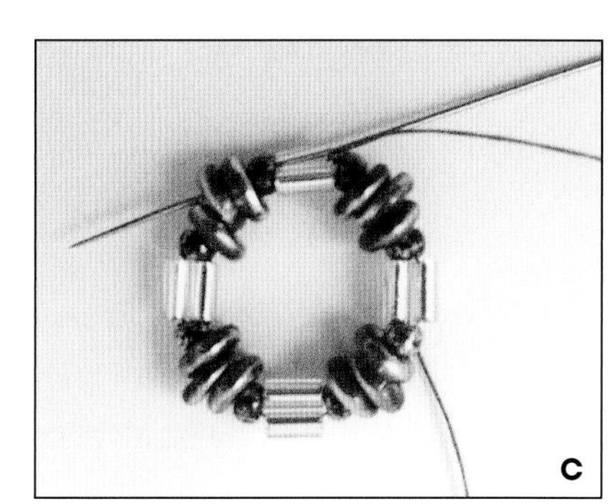
c

d

e

f

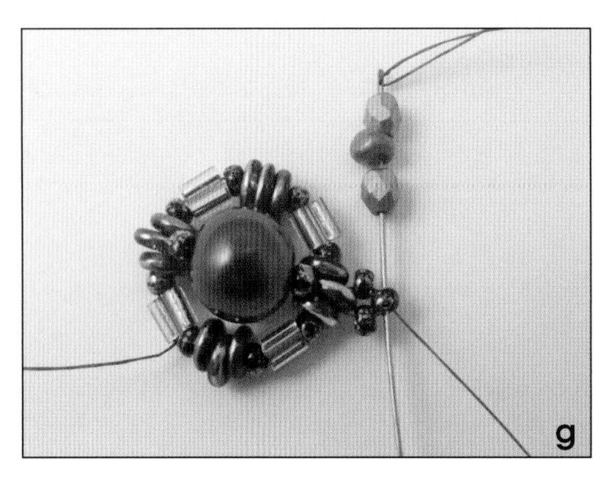
g

h

side of the ring **(photo d)**. Sew back through the 11º, pearl, and 11º added in this step. Continue through the center O-bead in the same direction.

4. Pick up three 11ºs, and sew through the O-bead your thread exited at the start of this step in the same direction **(photo e)**. Continue through the first two 11ºs picked up in this step **(photo f)**.

Connections

1. With the thread exiting the 11º in the previous component, pick up a 3mm fire-polished bead, a 3mm magatama, and a fire-polished bead. Sew back through the 11º your thread exited at the start of this step in the same direction **(photo g)**, and continue through the first fire-polished bead and magatama picked up in this step.

2. Pick up a fire-polished bead, an 11º, and a fire-polished bead, and sew through the magatama in the previous step. Continue through the first fire-polished bead and 11º picked up in this step.

3. Pick up an 11º, an O-bead, and an 11º, and sew back through the 11º your thread exited at the start of this step. Continue through the first 11º and the O-bead just added **(photo h)**.

Subsequent Components

1. Pick up an O-bead, an 11º, a bugle, an 11º, three O-beads, an 11º, a bugle, an 11º, three O-beads, an 11º, a bugle, an 11º, three O-beads, an 11º, a bugle, an 11º, and an O-bead, and sew through the O-bead your thread exited at the start of this step to form a ring. Retrace the thread path through the beads in this step **(photo i)**.

2. Sew through the next two beads to exit an 11º before a bugle, pick up a bugle, skip the bugle in the previous round, and sew through the next five beads. This bugle will sit on top of the bugle

i

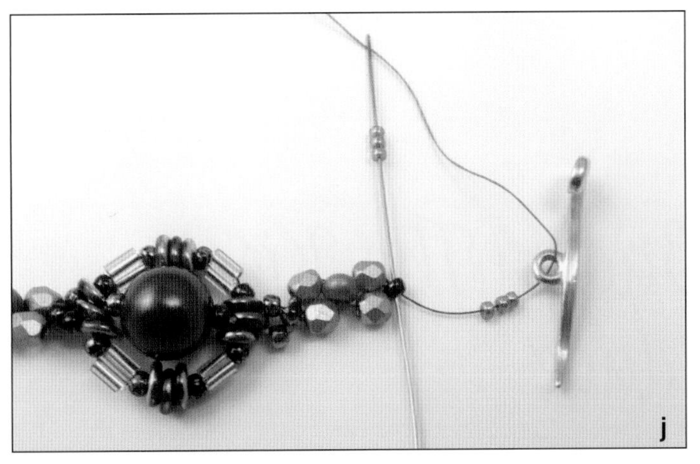

j

k

l

added in step 1. Repeat this step to complete the round.

3. Sew through the beads in the ring to exit a center O-bead in a group of three. Pick up an 11º, an 8mm glass pearl, and an 11º, and sew through the center O-bead in the group of three on the opposite side of the ring. Sew back through the 11º, pearl, and 11º added. Continue through the center O-bead.

4. Pick up three 11ºs, sew through the O-bead your thread exited at the start of this step in the same direction, and continue through the first two 11ºs picked up in this step.

5. Work as in steps 1–3 of "Connections" and then work steps 1–4 of "Subsequent Components" until you have a band the desired length, less 1 in. (2.5cm) for the clasp, ending with step 2 of "Connections." End and add thread (Basics) as needed.

Clasp and Embellishment

1. With the thread exiting an 11º, pick up three 15º seed beads, one half of the clasp, and three 15ºs, and sew back through the 11º your thread exited at the start of this step **(photo j)**. Retrace the thread path through the beads several times to secure, and exit the 11º. Do not end the working thread.

2. Sew through the nearest fire-polished bead, pick up three 11ºs, and sew through the next fire-polished bead **(photo k)**. Pick up an 11º, and sew through the next 11º, the center O-bead, and the next 11º. Pick up an 11º, and sew through the next fire-polished bead. Pick up three 11ºs, and sew through the next fire-polished bead **(photo l)**.

3. Sew through the beadwork to exit the center O-bead on the opposite side of the 8mm pearl. Work as in step 2 to embellish this connection between the two Flying Saucer Components. Repeat this step for the remaining connections in the bracelet.

4. Thread a needle on the tail and sew through the beadwork to exit the center O-bead at this end of the bracelet. Work as in steps 4 and 5 of "Subsequent Components" and then work as in steps 1 and 2 of "Clasp and Embellishment" to attach the other half of the clasp and embellish the connection. End the threads.

Il Bacio (The Kiss) Necklace

Two-hole beads are quite popular, and learning to use both holes to change direction and add dimension within your beadwork opens a wide range of design possibilities. This project introduces you to two-hole beads in a very simple, repetitive pattern, but the end result looks complicated and unique. Get comfortable with two-hole beads, and a whole new world of beading awaits you!

SUPPLIES

- 5g SuperDuos in each of **2** colors: A and B
- 2–3g 8º seed beads
- 3–4g 11º seed beads
- **2** 6mm jump rings
- Toggle clasp
- Beading needle #10
- Fireline, 6 lb. test
- **2** pairs of pliers

Necklace

1. Thread a needle on a comfortable length of thread. Pick up eight 11º seed beads and sew through the beads again to form a ring, leaving a 6-in. (15cm) tail. Retrace the thread path again and exit the first 11º.

2. Pick up two 11ºs, a color A SuperDuo, an 11º an A, an 11º, an A, an 11º, an A, five 11ºs, an A, an 11º, an A, an 11º, an A, an 11º, an A, and two 11ºs, and sew through the 11º your thread exited at the start of this step to form a ring **(photo a)**. Continue through the first 11º added in this step **(photo b)**.

3. Pick up two 11ºs, and sew through the available hole of the first A. Pick up an 8º seed bead, and sew through the available hole of the next A **(photo c)**. Pick up a color B SuperDuo, and sew through the available hole of the next A. Pick up an 8º seed bead, and sew through the available hole of the next A **(photo d)**.

a

b
c
d

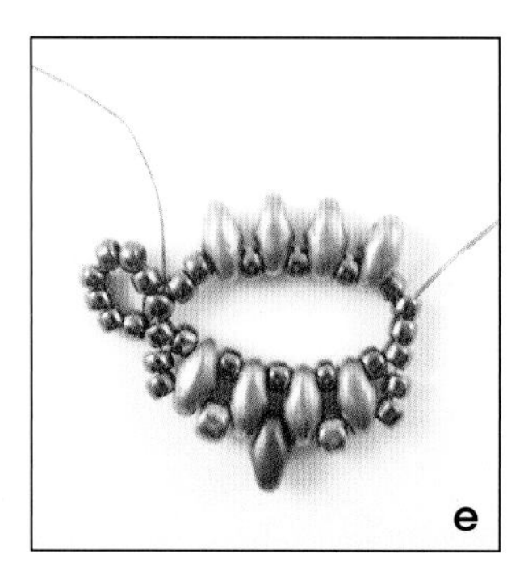

4. Pick up two 11ºs, skip the adjacent 11º, and sew through the next three 11ºs in the original ring **(photo e)**.

5. Work as in step 3 to embellish the other side of the ring. Pick up two 11ºs, skip the adjacent 11º, and sew through the next two 11ºs **(photo f)**.

6. Sew through the next three 11ºs and all the beads along this edge of the ring to exit the center 11º opposite the tail **(photo g)**.

7. Pick up three 11ºs, and sew through the 11º your thread exited at the start of this step **(photo h)**. Continue through the next two 11ºs added in this step to be in position to stitch the next component.

8. Work as in steps 2–7 until you have a band the desired length.

9. With the thread exiting an end 11º, pick up three 11ºs and sew through the 11º your thread exited at the start of this step. End the threads (Basics, p. 12).

10. Open a 6mm jump ring and attach the four-bead loop at one end of the necklace and one half of the clasp (Basics). Close the ring. Repeat on the other end of the necklace to attach the other half of the clasp.

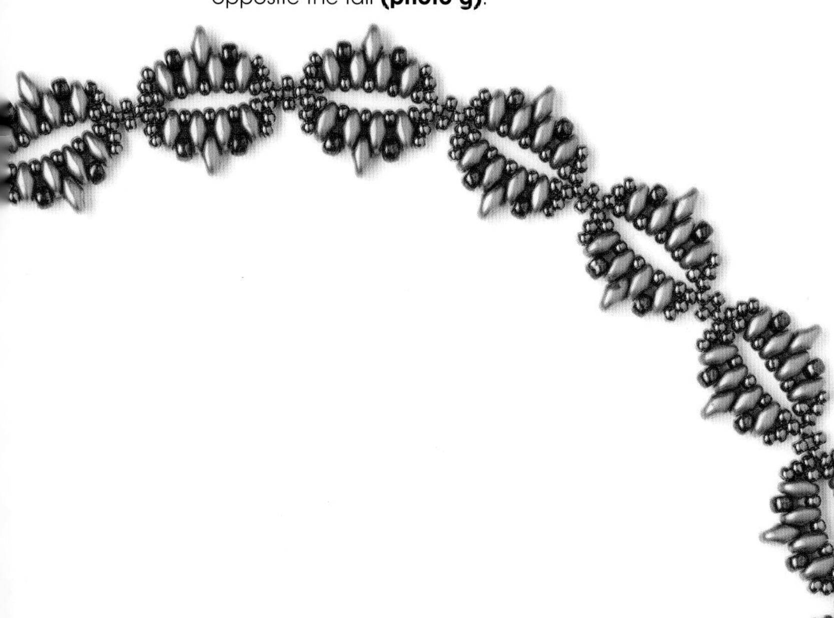

Natural Wonder Bracelet

Just because a bead has two holes in it doesn't mean you have to use both holes! SuperDuo beads make the perfect little aster-like flowers, and I love to connect them together to create long ropes. In this project, the central component is a three-colored square flower, while the straps are round florettes of the same three colors.

SUPPLIES

- **1** 6mm round glass bead
- 3g SuperDuos in each of **3** colors: A, B, and C
- 1g 8º seed beads
- 1g 11º seed beads
- **2** 6mm split rings
- Clasp
- Beading needle #10
- Fireline, 6 lb. test
- Split ring pliers and chainnose pliers

a

b

Center Component

1. On a comfortable length of thread, pick up a repeating pattern of an 11º seed bead and two color A SuperDuos four times, and tie the beads into a ring with a square knot (Basics, p. 12), leaving a 6-in. (15cm) tail. Sew through the beads again. Exit an 11º **(photo a)**.

2. Pick up a 6mm round bead, and sew through the 11º on the opposite side of the ring **(photo b)**. Sew back through the 6mm and the 11º your thread exited at

the start of this step **(photo c)**, and continue through the next A. Sew through the available hole in the A in the opposite direction **(photo d)**.

3. Pick up an 8º seed bead, and sew through the available hole in the next A (this will be the first A in the pair of As) **(photo e)**. Pick up two color B SuperDuos, and sew through the available hole in the next A to create a corner **(photo f)**. Repeat this step three times, and step up through the first 8º picked up in this step.

4. Pick up an 8º, and sew through the available hole in the next B. Pick up two color C SuperDuos, and sew through the available hole in the next B **(photo g)**. Pick up an 8º, sew through the next 8º, pick up an 8º, sew through the available hole in the next B, pick up two Cs, and sew through the available hole in the next B. Repeat this last stitch twice, and then pick up an 8º, sew through the 8º your thread exited at the start of this step, and continue through the first 8º picked up in this step **(photo h)**.

5. Pick up three 11ºs, an 8º, and three 11ºs, and sew through the last 8º picked up in the previous round in the same direction to make a loop. Continue through the adjacent 8º and the 8º your thread exited at the start of this step. Retrace the thread path several times.

6. Sew through the beadwork to exit an 8º picked up in step 4 opposite the loop created in this step. Work as in step 5 to create a loop on this side of the component **(photo i)**. End the threads (Basics).

Band of Flowers

1. First Flower: On a comfortable length of thread, pick up nine As and sew through the As again to form a ring. Retrace the thread path several times, then sew through the available hole of an A in the opposite direction.

2. Sew through the 8º picked up in step 5 or 6 of "Center Component," and sew through the available hole of the next A **(photo j)**. Sew through the inner hole of the same A in the opposite direction, and continue through the inner hole of the next five As in the ring to exit the A opposite the 8º. Sew through the available hole of this A in the opposite direction **(photo k)**.

3. Second Flower: Pick up seven Bs, and sew through the outer hole of the A your

thread exited at the start of this step **(photo l)**. Retrace the thread path several times and exit the inner hole of the fourth B picked up in this step (this will be the B that is opposite the A your thread exited at the start of this step **(photo m)**. Sew through the available hole in this B in the opposite direction **(photo n)**.

4. For subsequent flowers, work as in step 3, alternating the color of SuperDuos as follows: C, B, A, B, C for a 7-in. (18cm) bracelet. If you want to make a longer bracelet, add more flowers as needed. Note: Each "flower" adds approximately ½ in. (1.3cm) to the length.

5. Work as in steps 1–4 to make a mirror image for the band on the other side of the "Center Component."

Clasp

1. With the thread exiting the outer hole of the end SuperDuo, pick up five 11ºs and a 6mm split ring, and sew through all the beads again several times to secure. End the threads.

2. Using split ring pliers, open the split ring and attach one half of the clasp (Basics).

3. Work as in steps 1 and 2 for the other end of the band.

Light and Shadow Trifecta Bracelet

This classic bracelet is a study in color play. Contrasting colors or bead finishes meander gently among the pearls. Choose seed beads with subtle differences or go bold with a definite contrast. If you're short on time, make a single-strand bracelet. Once you get the hang of the color pattern, you'll move along quickly and can add multiple strands in an hour or two. If you're really ambitious, this makes a wonderful multi-strand necklace!

SUPPLIES

- **45** 5–6mm freshwater pearls
- 2g 8º seed beads
- 4g 11º seed beads in each of two colors: A and B
- 3-strand box clasp
- Beading needle #10
- Fireline, 6 lb. test
- **6** 4mm jump rings
- **2** pair of pliers

a

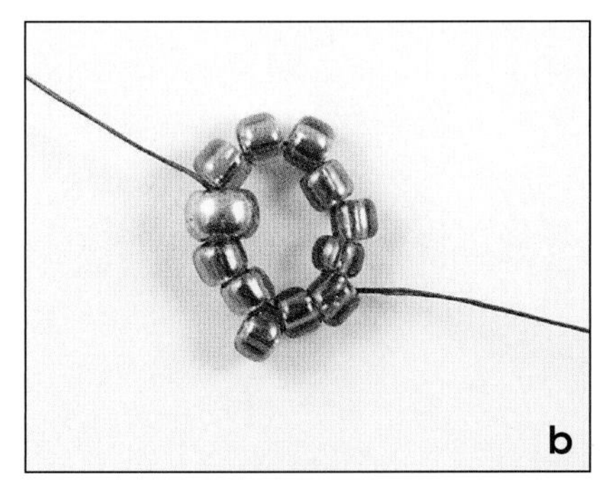
b

c

Beaded Pearl Strand

1. Thread a needle on 1 yd. (.9m) of thread. Pick up an 8º seed bead and 11 color A 11º seed beads and sew through all the beads to form a ring, leaving a 6-in. (15cm) tail. Tie a square knot with the tail (Basics, p. 12).

2. Continue through the first three beads **(photo a)**. Skip the next A in the ring, and sew through the following two As. Snug up the beads so the skipped A pops out **(photo b)**. Repeat the last stitch two times and retrace the thread path, skipping the popped-out As. Exit the 8º **(photo c)**.

3. Pick up three color B 11º seed beads, a 5–6mm pearl, and three As, and sew through the 8º again in the same direction **(photo d)**. Continue through the first three Bs and the pearl **(photo e)**.

4. Pick up three As, an 8º, and three Bs, and sew through the pearl again in the same direction. Sew through all the beads around the pearl again with a firm tension, and exit the 8º picked up in this step.

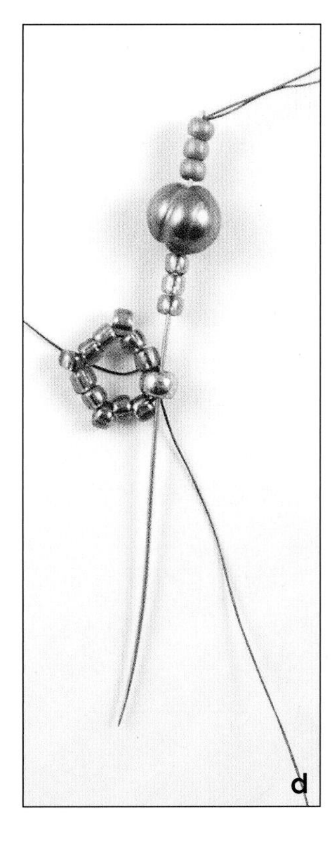
d

e

5. Pick up three As, a pearl, and three Bs, and sew through the 8º your thread exited at the start of this step. Continue through the As and the pearl **(photo f)**. Pick up three Bs, an 8º, and three As, and sew through the pearl in the same direction. Sew through all the beads around the pearl again with a firm tension, and exit the 8º picked up in this step **(photo g)**.

6. Work as in steps 4 and 5 for a total of 15 pearls.

7. Pick up 11 As, and sew through the 8º your thread exited at the start of this step. Work as in step 2 to create a bead loop at the end of the pearl band. End the threads (Basics).

8. Make two more beaded pearl strands.

Clasp

Open a 4mm jump ring (Basics) and attach the loop at one end of a beaded pearl strand and a loop on one half of the clasp. Close the ring. Repeat this step for each end of the bracelet, making sure the available end of the beaded pearl strand is attached to the corresponding loop on the remaining half of the clasp. It helps to connect both halves of the clasp as you go to make sure the strands are not crossed.

Designer's Note

If your pearls are closer to 6–7mm, pick up four 11ºs instead of three so the beads fully surround the pearl. If you're running short on time, make a single-strand bracelet, or add two loops of beads around each side of the pearl for a double-ringed, single-strand bracelet.

Chevron Chain Bracelet

Chevron chain is a form of netting (my second favorite stitch) and the best way to understand the stitch is to learn to "see" it. For me, the way to see the stitch is to do it over and over again. All of that aside, this is one of the most comfortable pieces of jewelry I wear. It's lightweight, drapes beautifully, and has a silky feel, almost like fabric. Start with two bands in your bracelet to get a feel for the technique, and then add a third, or even a fourth band for a real statement piece.

SUPPLIES

- 6g 11º seed bead in each of two colors: A and C
- 3g 8º seed beads in each of two colors: B and D
- **4** 4mm jump rings
- Tube clasp
- Beading needle #10
- Fireline, 6 lb. test
- **2** pairs of chainnose pliers

a

Band One

1. Thread a needle on a comfortable length of thread. Pick up six color A 11º seed beads and sew through all the beads again to form a ring. Retrace the thread path to secure **(photo a)**.

2. Pick up a color B 8º seed bead, an A, a B, two As,

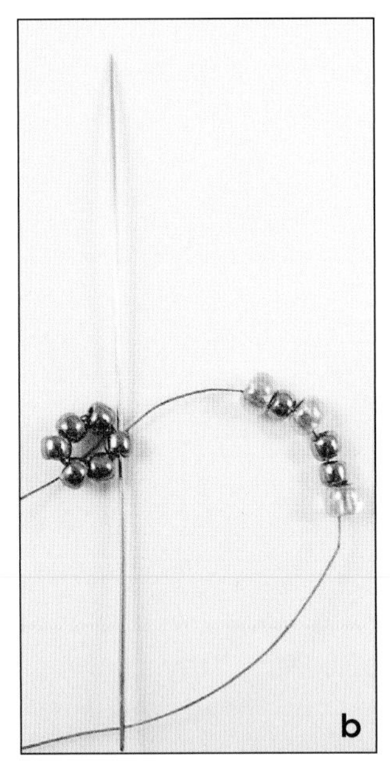
b

c

and a B, and sew through the A your thread exited at the start of this step **(photo b)**. Continue through the first B.

3. Pick up two As, a B, and an A, and sew through the next B picked up in the previous step **(photo c)**. Pick up two As, a B, and an A, and sew through the B picked up in this step in the opposite direction **(photo d)**.

4. Work as in step 3, ending and adding thread as needed (Basics, p. 12), until you have a band the desired length less ½ in. (1.3cm) for the clasp. Sew through the beadwork to exit the last A picked up in the previous step **(photo e)**.

5. Pick up five As, and sew through the first A again to form a ring **(photo f)**. Retrace the thread path several times to secure, and end the threads.

d

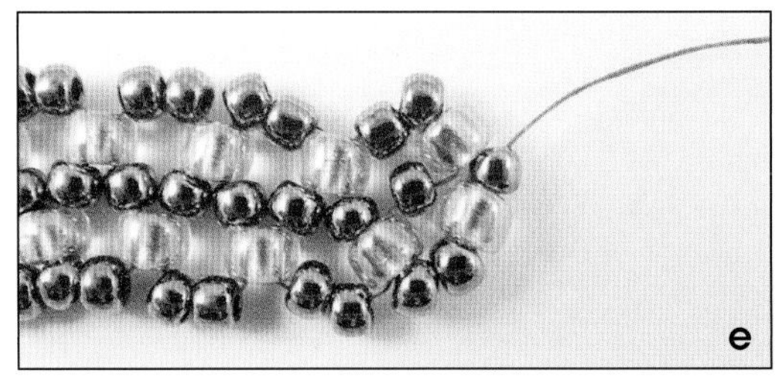
e

f

Band Two

Work as in steps 1–5, but use color C 11º seed beads in place of the As, and use color D 8º seed beads in place of the Bs.

Clasp

1. Using two pairs of pliers, open a 4mm jump ring and attach the loop at one end of a band to half of the clasp (Basics). Close the ring. Attach the other end of the band to the other half of the clasp the same way.

2. Repeat step 1 for the remaining band.

Designer's Notes

Don't worry if one band is slightly longer than the other. This stitch creates a draping bead fabric; you can twist the longer band before you secure the ends to the clasp to take up some of the slack.

Stitch multiple bands and attach them all to the same loop of the clasp for even more texture and interest.

tip

Attach one end of the band to the top loop on the first half of the clasp and the other end of the same band to the bottom loop on the second half of the clasp, and one band will cross the other when worn.

Tila for Two Bracelet

This fabulous bracelet uses two different two-hole beads: Tilas and half-Tilas. Work this project like you are building a brick wall or paving a walkway: back and forth, off-setting the holes and embellishing the edges as you go.

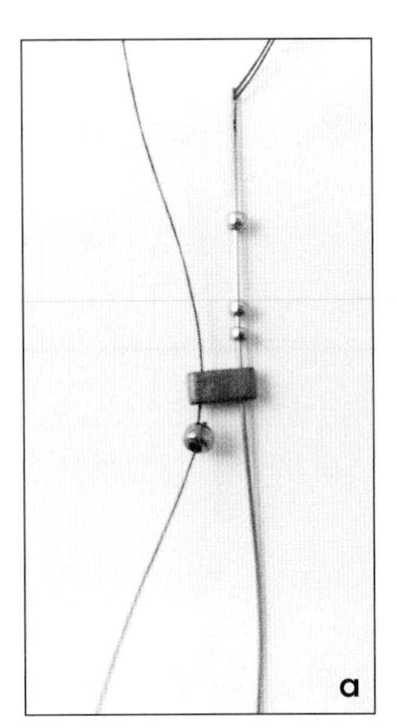
a

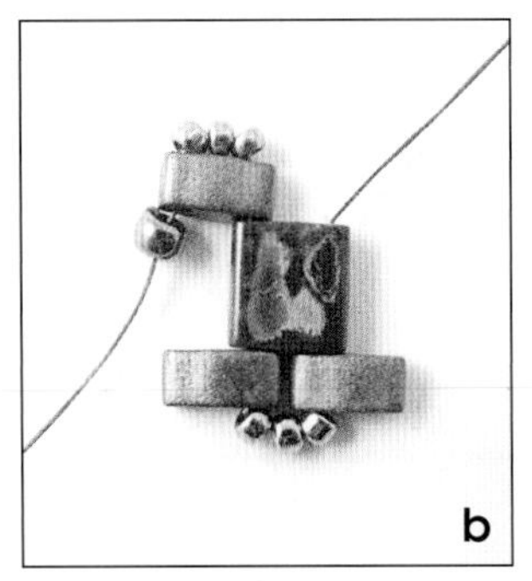
b

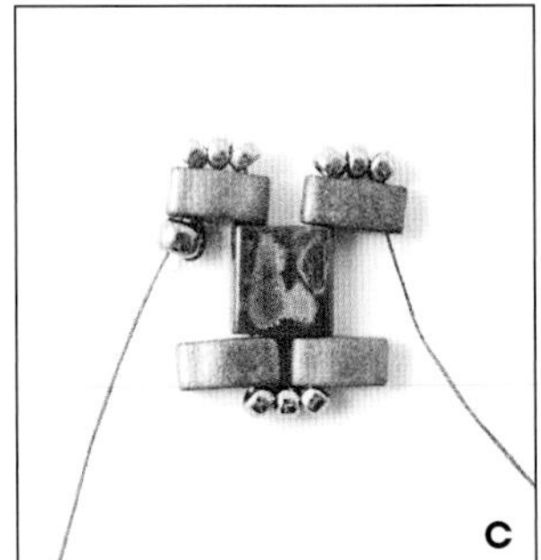
c

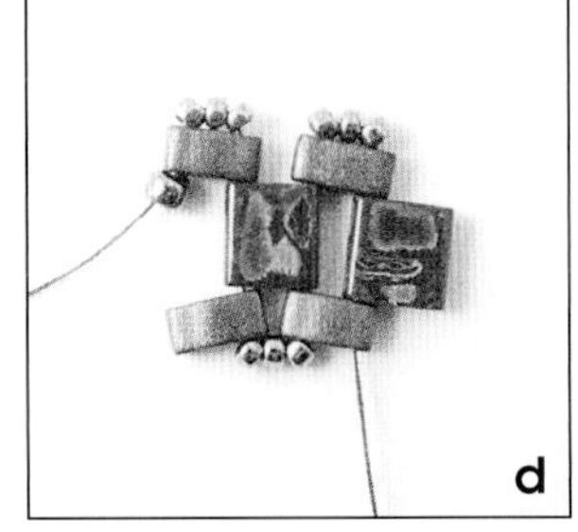
d

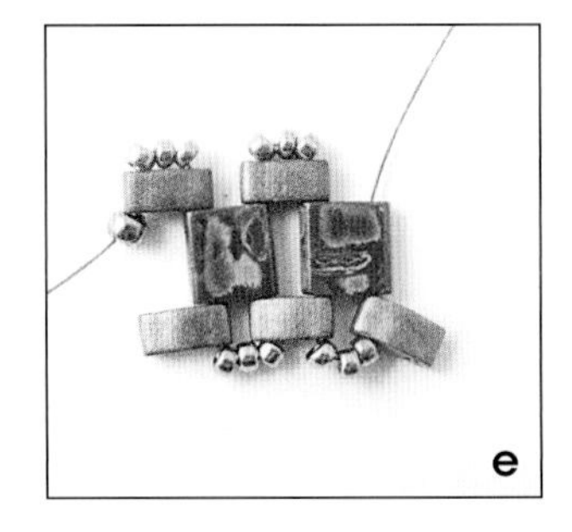
e

SUPPLIES

- **30** Tila beads
- **62** half-Tila beads
- 2g 15º seed beads
- **2** #3 bugle beads
- **2** 6mm soldered jump rings
- **2** 4mm jump rings
- Toggle clasp
- Beading needle, #11
- Fireline, 6 lb. test
- **2** pairs of chainnose pliers

Bracelet

1. Thread a needle and attach a stop bead on a comfortable length of thread (Basics, p. 12), leaving a 6-in. (15cm) tail. Pick up a half-Tila bead and three 15º seed beads, and sew through the available hole in the same half-Tila **(photo a)**. Pick up a Tila, a half-Tila, three 15ºs, and a half-Tila, and sew through the available hole in the Tila **(photo b)**.

2. Pick up a half-Tila and three 15ºs, and sew through the available hole in the same half-Tila **(photo c)**. Pick up a Tila, and sew through the available hole in the nearest half-Tila on the other edge of the band **(photo d)**.

3. Pick up three 15ºs and a half-Tila, and sew through the available hole of the nearest Tila **(photo e)**.

4. Continue working as in steps 2 and 3 until you have a band ½ in. (1.3cm) longer than your wrist measurement, ending and adding thread as needed (Basics). The length of the band will shorten up as you work the remaining steps.

5. Pick up a half-Tila and three 15ºs, and sew through the available hole in the same half-Tila **(photo f)**. Pick up a 15º, a #3 bugle bead, a 15º, and a 6mm soldered jump ring, and sew through the available hole in the half-Tila along the other edge of the band **(photo g)**.

6. Pick up two 15ºs and sew through the last 15º before the other hole in the same half-Tila. Continue through the beads to exit the first 15º on the other edge of the band **(photo h)**.

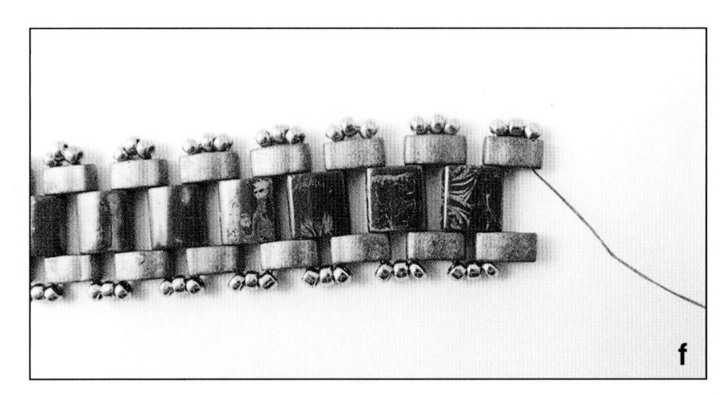
f

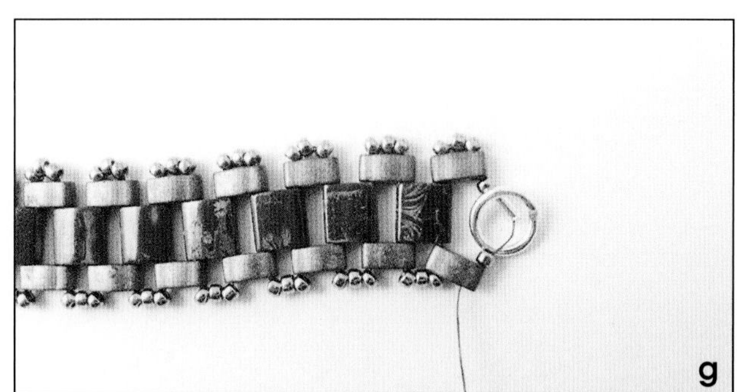
g

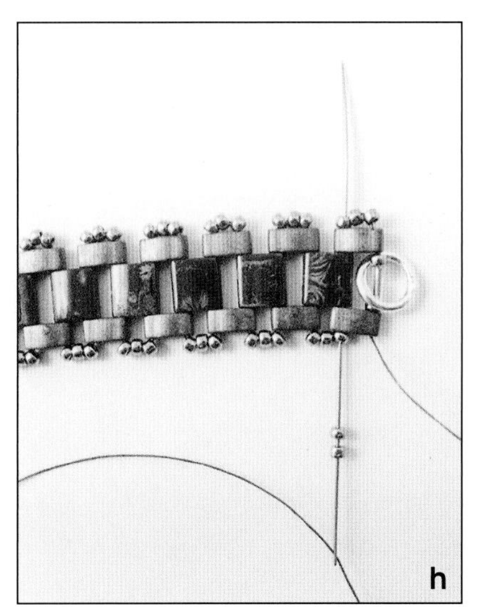
h

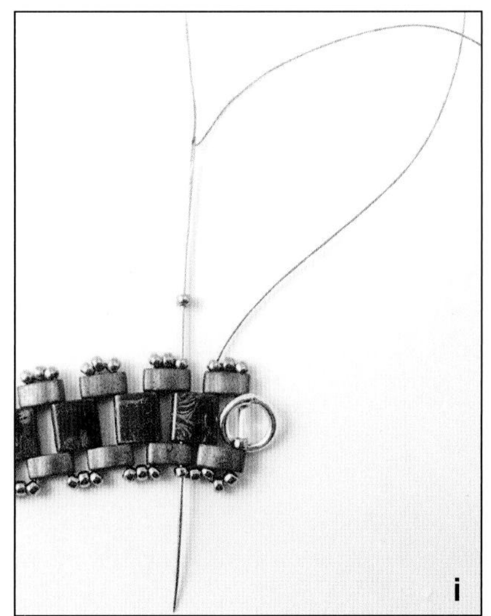
i

j

k

7. Pick up a 15º and sew down through the 15º before the hole in the adjacent half-Tila, working toward the tail. Continue through the beads to exit the first 15º along the other edge of the band **(photo i)**. Repeat this step for the length of the bracelet until you reach the end half-Tila that does not have three edge 15ºs **(photo j)**.

8. With the thread exiting the first 15º in the last set on this edge of the band, pick up two 15ºs, and sew through the available hole in the half-Tila **(photo k)**. Pick up a 15º, a #3 bugle bead, a 15º, and a 6mm soldered jump ring, and sew through the nearest hole of the half-Tila on the other edge of the band. Continue through the three 15ºs, the half-Tila, Tila, and the 15º your thread exited at the start of this step. Remove the stop bead and retrace the thread path through the beads added in this step twice to secure. End the threads (Basics).

9. Open a 4mm jump ring and attach the soldered jump ring and one half of the clasp (Basics). Close the ring. Repeat this step for the other end of the bracelet and the remaining half of the clasp.

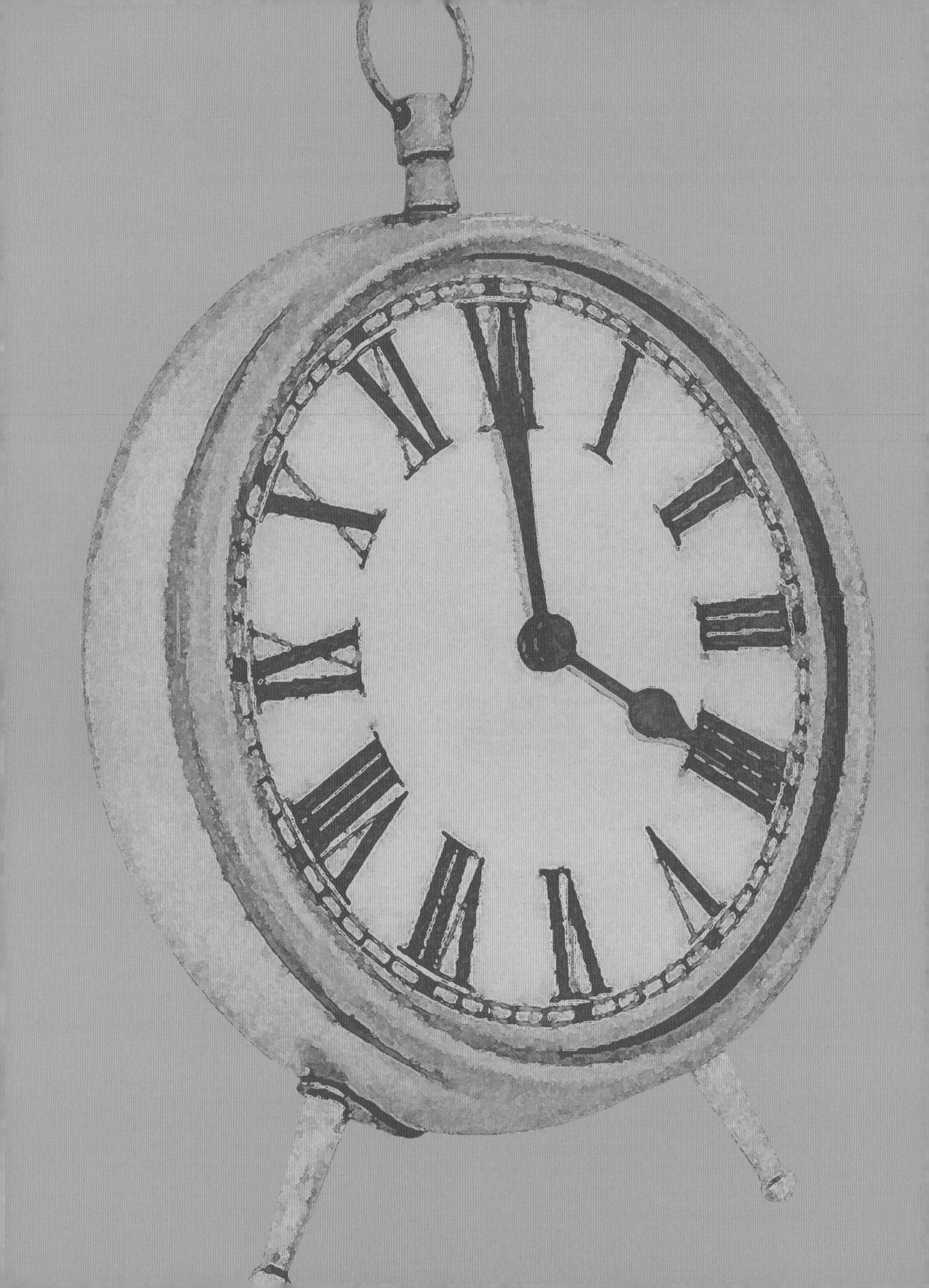

4 HOUR *Projects*

Captured Pearls Necklace

Double rings around each pearl give this necklace the look of fine jewelry. Two-sided crystal florets add a delicious sparkle to the piece as well.

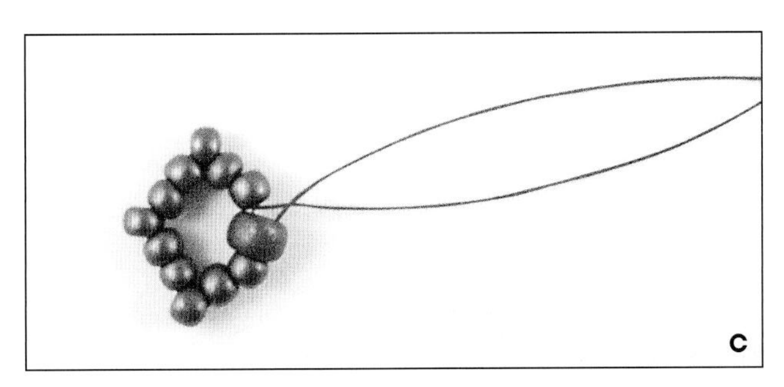

SUPPLIES

- **36** 5–6mm pearls
- **28** 4mm bicone crystals
- 2g 8º seed beads
- 6g 11º seed beads
- **2** 6mm jump rings
- Clasp
- Beading needle #10
- Fireline, 6 lb. test
- **2** pairs of pliers

Make the Necklace

1. Thread a needle on a comfortable length of thread. Pick up an 8º seed bead and 11 color A 11º seed beads, and tie a square knot with the tail (Basics, p. 12) to form a ring, leaving a 6-in. (15cm) tail. Sew through the 8º, the next two As, skip the next A, and sew through the following two As **(photo a)**. Snug up the beads so the skipped A pops out **(photo b)**. (You may have to help the bead pop out with your needle.) Skip the next A, and sew through the following two As. Snug up the beads so the skipped A pops out. Repeat the last stitch, snug

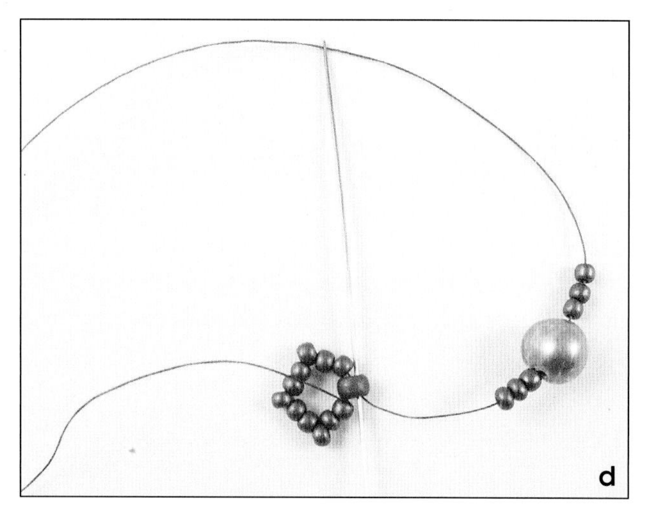

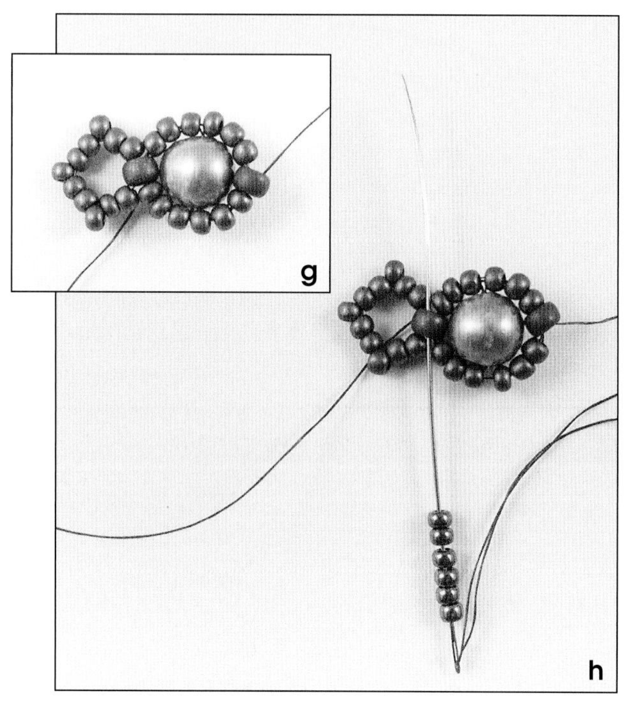

up the beads, and continue through the 8º **(photo c)**.

2. Pick up three As, a 6mm pearl, and three As, and sew through the 8º in the same direction **(photo d)**. Continue through the first three As and the pearl again **(photo e)**. The beads will form a loop around one half of the pearl.

3. Pick up three As, an 8º, and three As, and sew through the 6mm pearl in the same direction **(photo f)**. These beads will form a loop around the other half of the pearl. Sew through all the beads around the pearl, using a firm tension. Sew through the beads to exit the 8º picked up in this step **(photo g)**.

4. Pick up six or seven color B 11ºs and sew through the 8º opposite the 8º your thread exited at the start of this step **(photo h)**. This forms a double loop of beads around one half of the pearl. Push this new loop of beads behind the loop already around the pearl. **Photo i** shows the other side of the pearl. Repeat this step to form a second loop of Bs around the other half of the pearl. Sew through all the beads in this step, and exit the 8º your thread exited at the start of this step **(photo j)**.

5. Work as in steps 2–5 twice to create two more pearl components.

6. With the thread exiting the end 8º in a pearl component, pick up an A, a 4mm bicone crystal, an A, a 4mm, an A, an 8º, an A, and a 4mm **(photo k)**. Skip

k

l

m

n

the last five beads just picked up, and sew back through the next A **(photo l)**. Snug up the beads **(photo m)**. Pick up a 4mm and an A, and sew through the 8º your thread exited at the start of this step in the same direction. Sew through the first six beads added at the start of this step to exit the 8º **(photo n)**.

7. Work as in steps 2–4 five times and then work as in step 6, ending and adding thread as needed (Basics).

8. Work step 7 five times, and then work steps 2–4 three times.

9. Pick up 11 As, and sew through the 8º your thread exited at the start of this step. Continue through the next two As, skip the following A, and sew through the next two As. Snug up the beads so the skipped A pops out. Skip the next A, and sew through the following two As. Snug up the beads so the skipped A pops out. Repeat the last stitch, and snug up the beads. Retrace the thread path through the beads in this step, and end the threads.

10. Open a 6mm jump ring (Basics) and attach the loop at one end of the necklace and one half of the clasp. Close the ring. Repeat on the other end of the necklace with the other half of the clasp.

Designer's Note

This is a really easy design to customize and there is really no right or wrong in terms of the number of beads. The pearls I used in the copper and green necklace were closer to 6-7mm in diameter so I used a total of seven 11ºs around each half of the larger pearls rather than the six 11ºs in the instructions above. Experiment with the number of beads in each loop around the pearl to find the look you like the best. Also, in the green necklace, I added six pearls between each bicone crystal cluster rather than five as in the instructions just to make it slightly different from the silver/purple necklace.

Fishnet Stockings Rope

You'll find this rope, like a thick silver or gold chain, to be a wardrobe staple. The netting stitch creates a necklace that is supple, and using two different colors of beads creates a beautiful accessory that can stand on its own or display a pendant.

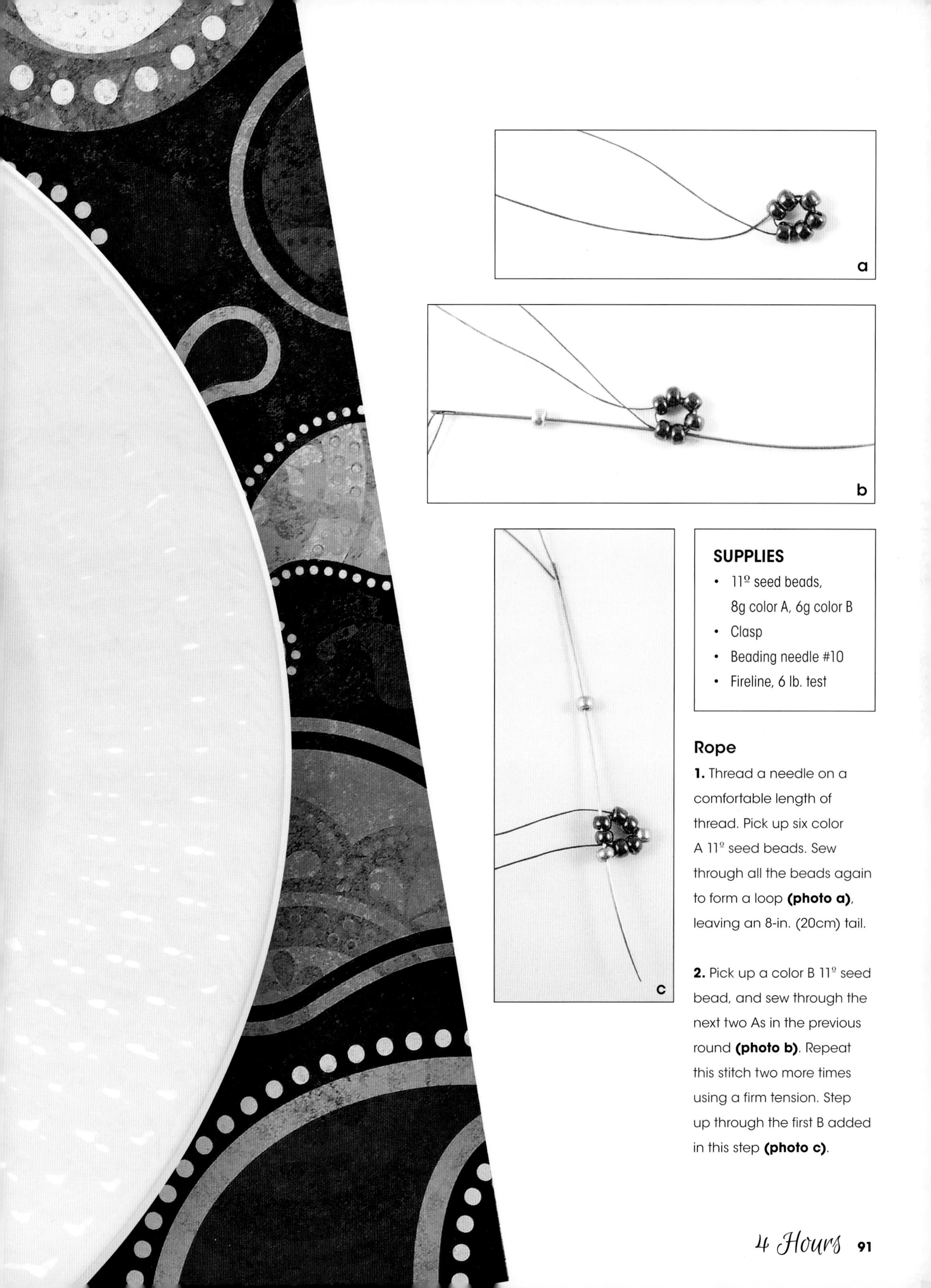

SUPPLIES

- 11° seed beads, 8g color A, 6g color B
- Clasp
- Beading needle #10
- Fireline, 6 lb. test

Rope

1. Thread a needle on a comfortable length of thread. Pick up six color A 11° seed beads. Sew through all the beads again to form a loop **(photo a)**, leaving an 8-in. (20cm) tail.

2. Pick up a color B 11° seed bead, and sew through the next two As in the previous round **(photo b)**. Repeat this stitch two more times using a firm tension. Step up through the first B added in this step **(photo c)**.

Due to the open weave of the netting stitch, even a beginner can stitch an 18-in. (46cm) rope in 4 hours or less.

d

g

e

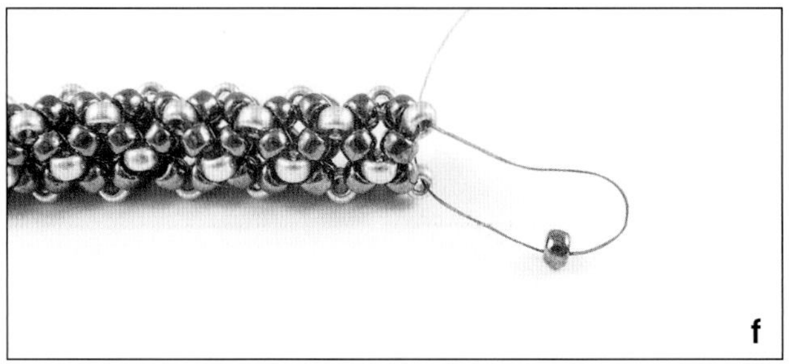
f

3. Pick up two As and sew through the next B in the previous step **(photo d)**. Repeat this stitch two more times using a firm tension so the beadwork begins to cup and form a tube. Step up through the first A added in this step **(photo e)**.

4. Work as in steps 2 and 3, ending and adding thread (Basics, p. 12) as necessary, until you have a rope the desired length, minus 1 in. (2.5cm) for the clasp. Be sure to end with step 2.

5. Pick up an A and sew through the next B in the previous round **(photo f)**. Repeat this stitch two more times and step up through the first A added in this step.

6. Pick up an A and sew through the next A from the previous step. Repeat this stitch two more times and step up through the first A added in this step.

7. Work as in step 6 and then sew through all three As added in this step several times using a firm tension.

8. Pick up nine As and the loop of one half of the clasp. Sew through another A added in step 7, and the A your thread exited at the start of this step **(photo g)**. Retrace the thread path through the loop several times. End the working thread (Basics).

9. Thread a needle on the tail and work as in steps 5–8. End the tail.

Designer's Note

For a thicker rope, pick up eight color A 11º seed beads in step 1, and then add one extra repeat in steps 2–6, or substitute 8º seed beads in two colors in place of the 11ºs for a more substantial necklace.

Pearls à la Mode Choker

The pearls take center stage in this delicate choker, with the crystals, Minos, and 11ºs providing the perfect accompaniment for a beautiful necklace. While dainty looking in your hands, it makes a big impact lying gracefully at the base of your neck. I use an extender chain to adjust the length of the choker, depending on the neckline of my outfit. Tension is key in this project—don't pull too tight, or it will bunch together. Be sure to check the tension before tying any knots or ending your threads!

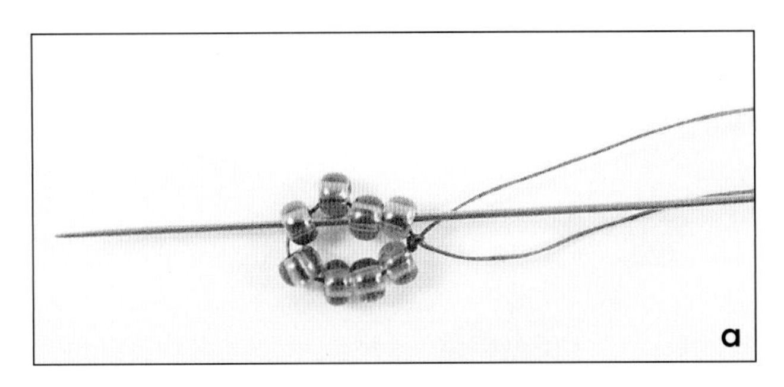

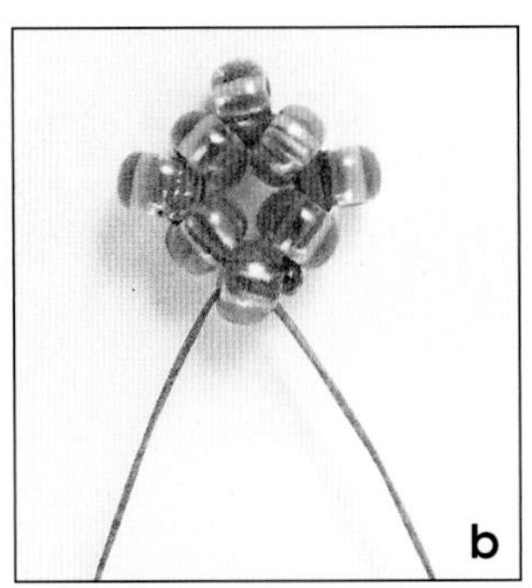

SUPPLIES

- **40–46** 4x6mm glass pearls
- **40–46** 3mm bicone crystals
- 2–3g 2.5x3mm Minos beads
- 3g 11º seed beads color A
- 1g 11º seed beads color B
- **2** 6mm jump rings
- 2 in. (5cm) extender chain
- Lobster claw clasp
- Beading needle #11
- Fireline, 6 lb. test
- **2** pairs of chainnose pliers

Choker

1. Thread a needle on a comfortable length of thread. Pick up eight color A 11º seed beads and tie the beads into a ring with a square knot (Basics, p. 12), leaving a 6-in. (15cm) tail.

2. Sew through the first two As, skip the next A, and sew through the following A **(photo a)**. Snug up the beads so the skipped A pops out. Skip the next A and sew through the following A. Snug up the beads so the skipped A pops out. Skip the next A, sew through the following two As, and snug up the beads. The thread will be exiting the first A picked up in step 1 **(photo b)**.

3. Pick up three As, a 4x6mm pearl, and three As, and sew back through the A your thread exited at the start of this step **(photo c)**. Continue through the first three As and the pearl picked up in this step **(photo d)**.

4. Pick up three As, a color B 11º seed bead, and three As, and sew through the pearl **(photo e)**. Continue through the first seven beads picked up in this step.

5. Pick up a B, and sew through the next seven As picked up in step 3 **(photo f)**. Pick up a 3mm bicone crystal and sew through the next three As and the B picked up in step 4 **(photo g)**.

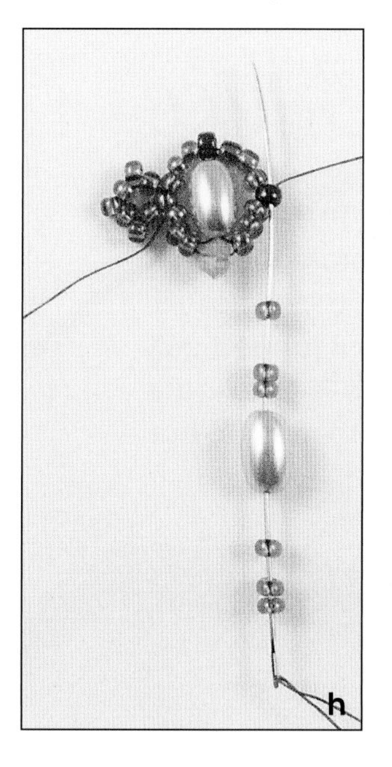

6. Pick up three As, a pearl, and three As, and sew through the B your thread exited at the start of this step **(photo h)**. Continue through the first three As and the pearl.

7. Work as in steps 4–6, ending and adding thread as necessary (Basics), until you have a band the desired length minus 1 in. (2.5cm) for the clasp, ending with step 5.

8. With the thread exiting the last B in the previous stitch, pick up seven As and sew through the B your thread exited at the start of this step. Continue through the first A picked up in this step.

9. Skip the next A and sew through the following A. Snug up the beadwork so the skipped A pops out. Skip the next A and sew through the following A. Snug up the beads so the skipped A pops out. Skip the next A and sew through the following A and B. Snug up the beads, and end the threads.

10. Attach 1 yd. (.9m) of thread (Basics) to one end of the necklace. Sew through the beadwork to exit the B at the top of the end pearl **(photo i)**. Pick up an A, a 2.5x3mm Minos bead, and an A, and sew through the B at the top of the next pearl **(photo j)**. Repeat the last stitch for the length of the band, gently snugging up the beads so the necklace has a slight curve. Sew through the beadwork to exit the last B with your needle pointing in the opposite direction. Sew through all the beads in this step again to secure, tying a couple of half-hitch knots between the beads (Basics). End the threads.

11. Open a 6mm jump ring and attach the loop at one end of the necklace and the end link of an extender chain **(photo k)** (Basics). Close the ring.

12. Open a 6mm jump ring and attach the available loop at the other end of the necklace and the loop of the remaining half of the clasp. Close the ring.

Designer's Notes

If you do not have Minos beads, you can easily replace them with 3mm crystals or fire-polished beads. Just make sure you do not snug up the beads in step 10 too much, or your work will bunch up. You want to achieve a gentle curve.

Make a complementary bracelet by substituting 3mm crystals in place of the Bs added at the start of step 5 so you have crystals at each end of the pearl. Skip step 10, and add a toggle clasp rather than the extender chain and lobster claw clasp.

Sophia's Fandango Necklace

In this necklace, small dagger beads fan out from the bottom of each pearl like a dancer's skirt swinging out as she moves. This project is for my daughter because when she was little, she chose her dresses based on how "twirly" the skirt was. She would only wear those that fanned out appropriately as she spun around in a circle. The neckstrap is a delicate embellished flat herringbone stitch, which is not only easy to master, but adds texture and interest to your beadwork.

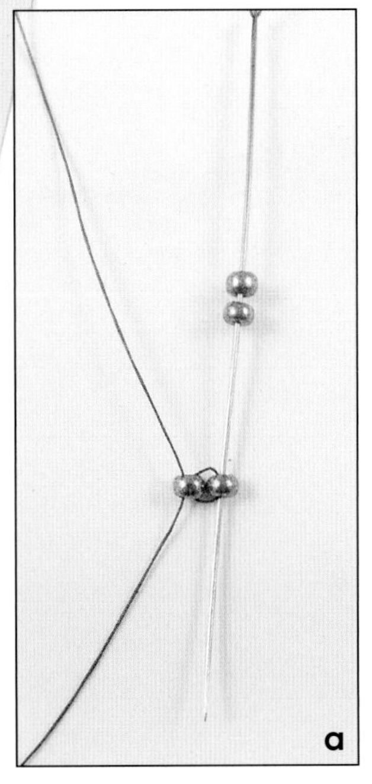

Necklace

1. Thread a needle on a comfortable length of thread. Pick up two color A 11º seed beads and sew through the first A again in the same direction, leaving an 8-in. (20cm) tail. The two beads will line up side by side to form two columns of beads with their holes parallel.

2. Pick up two As and sew down through the A in the second column **(photo a)**. Sew up through the adjacent A in the first column, and continue through the first A picked up in this step to be in position for the next step.

3. Pick up two As and sew down through the adjacent A in the second column, pick up a color B 11º seed bead, and sew up through the last two As in the first column **(photo b)**. The B will sit on top of your work in the center between the two columns of As.

4. Work as in step 2 three times, then work as in step 3

SUPPLIES

- **55** 3x12 mm dagger beads
- **11** 6mm pearls
- **12** 3mm pearls
- 3g 11º seed beads color A
- 1g 11º seed beads color B
- **2** 6mm jump rings
- Box clasp
- Beading needle #11
- Fireline, 6 lb. test
- **2** pairs of chainnose pliers

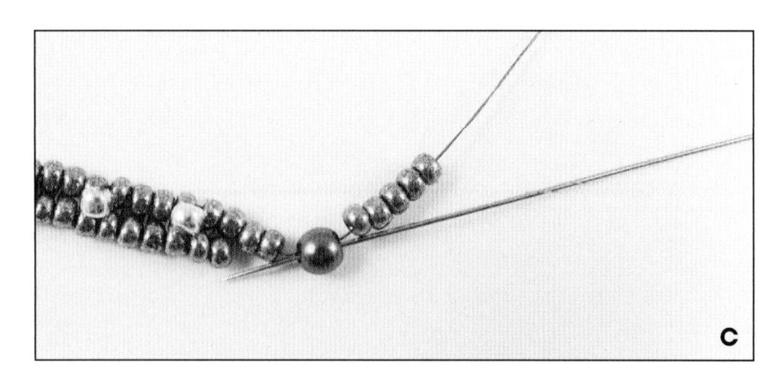

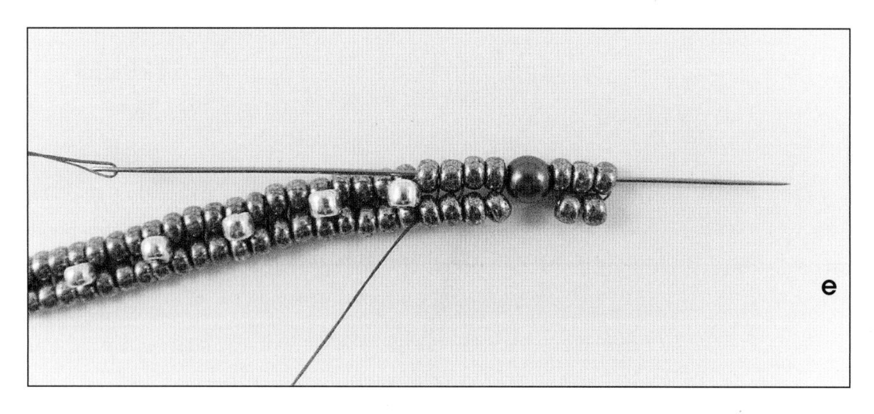

until you have a strip that measures approximately 3¼ in. (8.3cm) long, ending and adding thread as needed (Basics, p. 12).

5. Pick up two As, a 3mm pearl, and five As, and sew back through the 3mm in the opposite direction **(photo c)**. Pick up two As, and sew down through the next two beads in the second column **(photo d)**. Sew up through the corresponding As in the first column, and continue through the two As, 3mm, and next three As picked up in this step **(photo e)**.

6. Pick up seven As, a 6mm pearl, and an A, and sew through the A your thread exited at the start of this step in the same direction **(photo f)**. The new As will form a loop around one half of the 6mm. Continue through the first seven As and the 6mm picked up in this step **(photo g)**.

7. Pick up an A, five dagger beads, and an A, and sew through the 6mm with the needle pointing toward the tail. Push these beads to the available side of the pearl **(photo h)**. Sew through the nine As around the pearl and the five dagger beads. Continue through the follow-

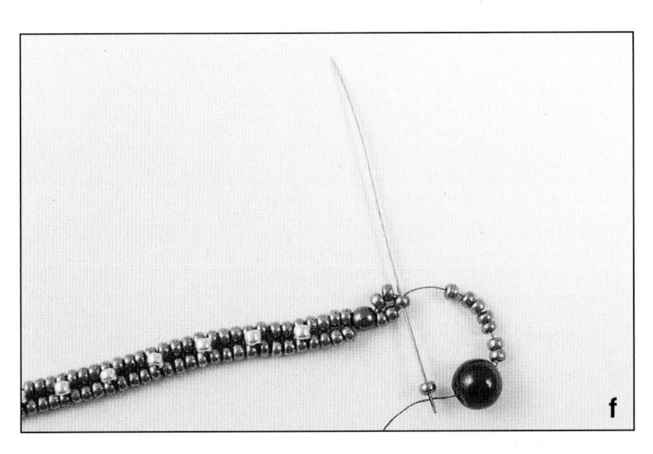

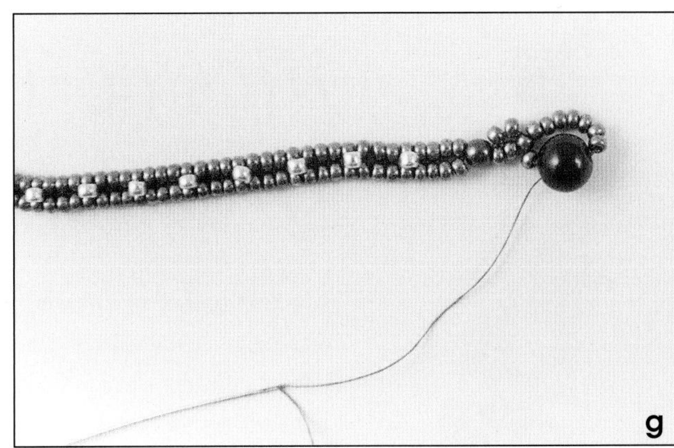

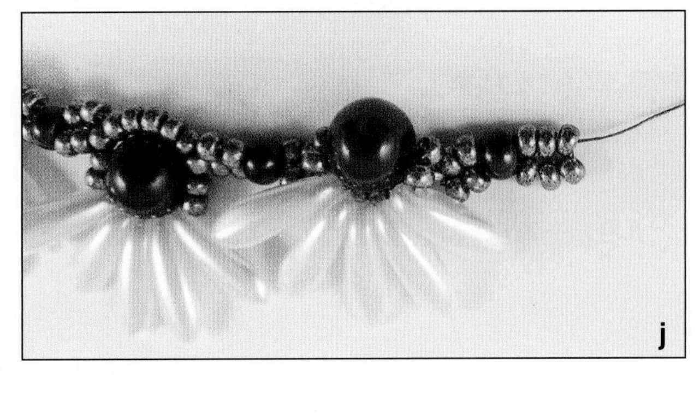

ing As, to exit the sixth A picked up at the start of step 6 as shown in **photo i**.

8. Pick up two As, a 3mm pearl, and five As, and sew back through the 3mm in the opposite direction. Pick up two As, and sew through the A your thread exited at the start of this step. Continue through the first two As, the pearl, and the next three As.

9. Work as in steps 6–8 for a total of 11 dagger/pearl components, ending and adding thread as needed (Basics), and end with step 7.

10. With the thread exiting the sixth A, pick up two As, a 3mm, and six As, and sew back through the 3mm. Pick up two As, sew through the A your thread exited at the start of this step, and continue through the first two As, 3mm, and following three As picked up in this step **(photo j)**.

11. Work as in step 4 on this end of the necklace.

12. Pick up five As, and sew through the next four As in the other column to form a loop at the end of the neck-lace, and then sew up through the corresponding As in the first column. Retrace the thread path through the beads in this step several times, tying a couple of half-hitch knots between the beads (Basics). End the working thread.

13. Open a 6mm jump ring and attach the end loop and one half of the clasp (Basics). Close the ring.

14. Thread a needle on the tail and work as in steps 12 and 13 on this end of the necklace.

Mosaic Rivoli Bracelet

This bracelet incorporates crystal rivolis, two-hole cabochon beads, pearls, and DiamonDuos in a kaleidoscope of colors. Not too ostentatious, but with a fair amount of bling, this bracelet will become the piece you reach for on date nights and other special occasions. This project is good practice in the art of seamlessly joining components and embellishing those joins for a cohesive design.

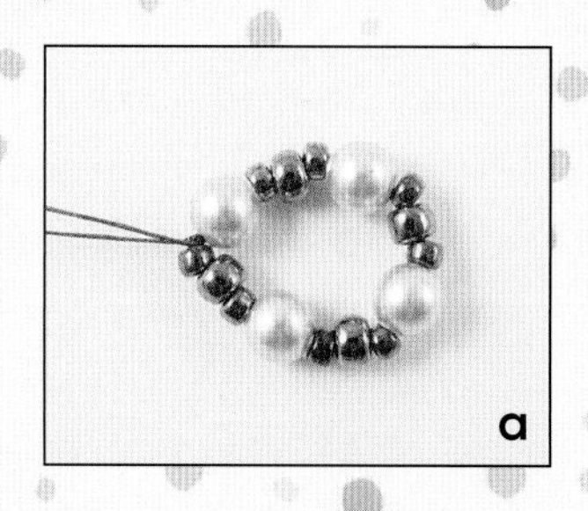

a

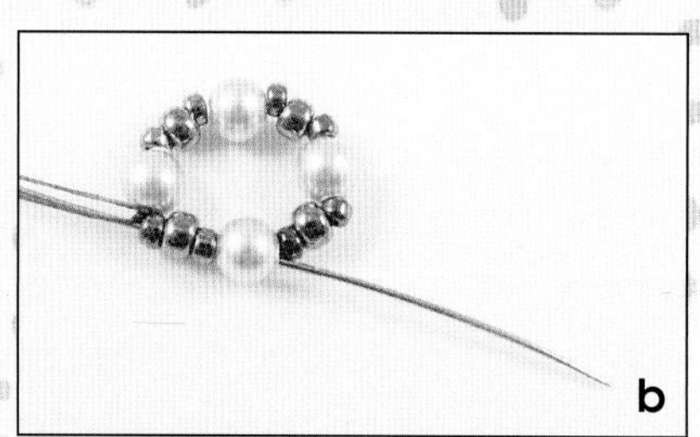

b

c

Rivoli and Cabochon Component

1. Thread a needle on 2 ft. (61cm) of thread. Pick up a repeating pattern of a 15° seed bead, an 11° seed bead, a 15°, and a color C 3mm pearl for a total of four pearls. Tie the beads into a ring with a square knot (Basics, p. 12), leaving an 8-in. (20cm) tail **(photo a)**. Sew through all the beads again and continue through the first 15°, 11°, 15°, and pearl **(photo b)**.

SUPPLIES

- **2** 12mm rivolis in each of two colors: A and B
- **5** 8mm two-hole cabochons
- 16 5x8mm DiamonDuos
- **8** 3mm glass or crystal pearls in each of two colors: C and D
- 2g 3mm magatamas
- 3g 11º seed beads
- 2g 15º seed beads
- **2** 4mm jump rings
- Clasp
- Beading needle #10
- Fireline, 6 lb. test
- **2** pairs of chainnose pliers

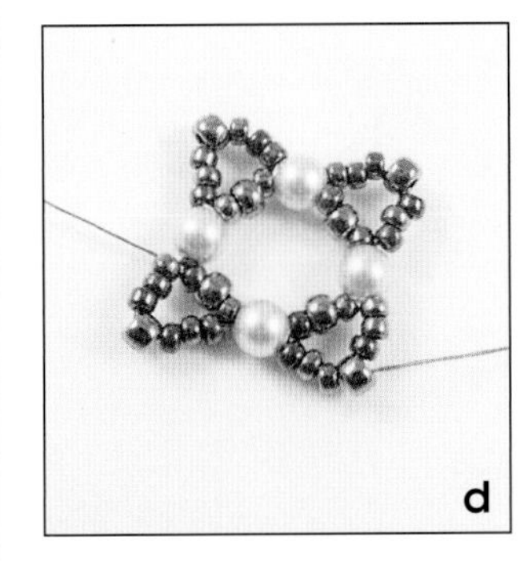
d

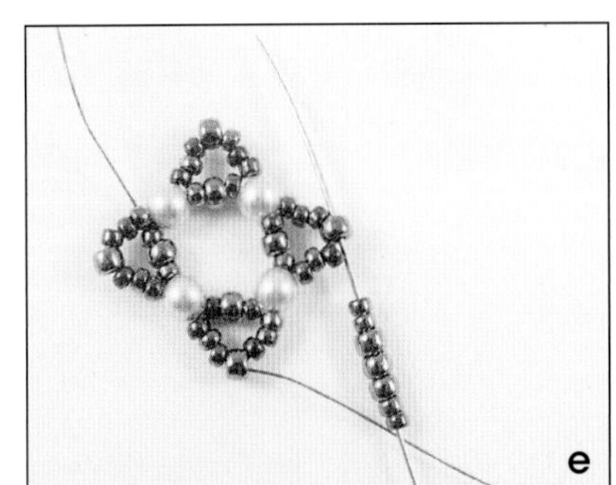
e

f

g

h

i

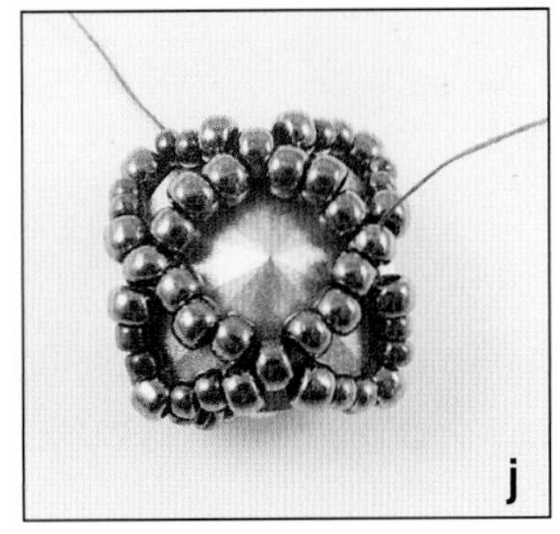
j

k

l

2. Pick up three 15ºs, an 11º, and three 15ºs, and sew through the next pearl in the ring **(photo c)**. Repeat this step three times, and step up through the first three 15ºs and 11º to be in position for the next step **(photo d)**.

3. Pick up two 15ºs, three 11ºs, and two 15ºs, and sew through the next 11º added in the previous step **(photo e)**. Repeat this step three more times, and step up through the first two 15ºs and two 11ºs added in this step to be in position for the next step **(photo f)**.

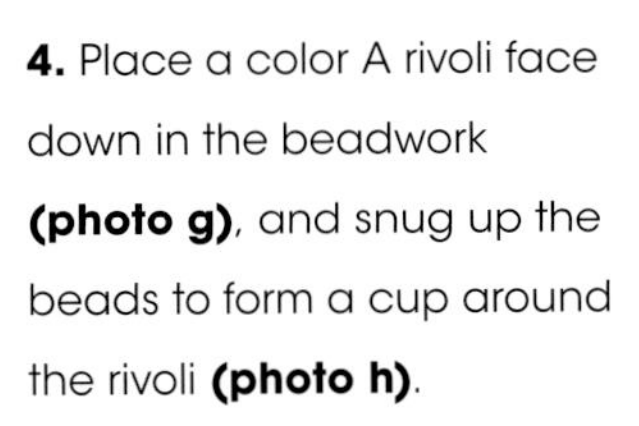

4. Place a color A rivoli face down in the beadwork **(photo g)**, and snug up the beads to form a cup around the rivoli **(photo h)**.

5. Pick up three 11ºs, and sew through the center 11º in the next three-11º set in the previous round. Snug up the beads **(photo i)**. Repeat this stitch three more times using a firm tension to secure the rivoli in the beadwork. **Photo j** shows the back of the beadwork. **Photo k** shows the front.

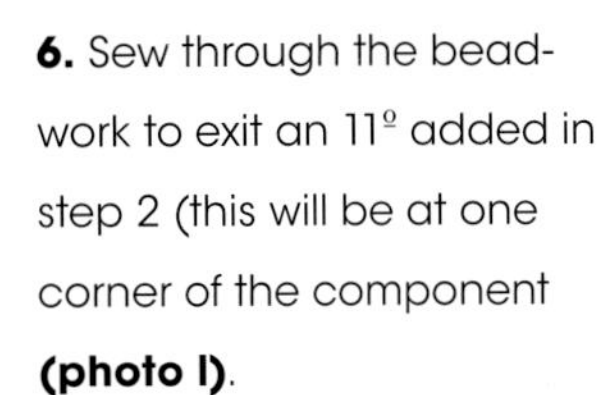

6. Sew through the beadwork to exit an 11º added in step 2 (this will be at one corner of the component **(photo l)**.

7. Pick up three 11ºs, a magatama, two 5x8mm DiamonDuos (making sure

m

n

o

p

q

r

s

t

they are both facing up as in **photo m**), a magatama, and three 11ºs, and sew through the next corner 11º **(photo n)**.

8. Without adding any beads, sew through the beadwork to exit an available corner 11º **(photo o)**. Work as in step 7.

9. Sew through the beadwork to exit the second DiamonDuo picked up in step 7 **(photo p)**. Pick up an 11º, a magatama, and an 11º, and sew through the available hole in the same DiamonDuo **(photo q)** with your needle pointing in the opposite direction. Pick up an 8mm two-hole cabochon, making sure it is right-side up in relation to the rest of the component **(photo r)**, and sew through the available hole of the adjacent DiamonDuo **(photo s)**. Pick up an 11º, a magatama, and an 11º, and sew through the other hole in the same DiamonDuo **(photo t)**. Retrace the thread path through all the beads in this step.

10. Sew through the beadwork to exit the second DiamonDuo added in step 8, and work as in step 9. Do not end the threads. This completes one component.

Subsequent Components

Work as in steps 1–10, alternating color A and B rivolis

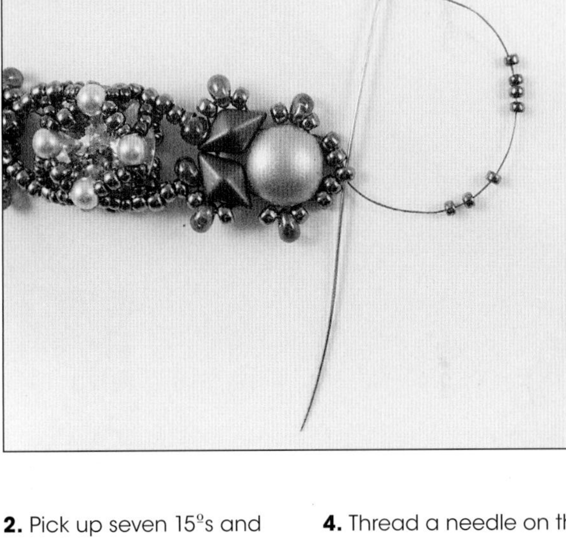

and color C and D 3mm pearls, but in step 10, instead of picking up a new two-hole cabochon, sew through the available holes of a cabochon in the previous component **(photo u)**. For a 7½-in. (19.1cm) bracelet, make a total of four components and embellish the cabochon as in "Joining Embellishment," below.

Joining Embellishment

1. With the thread exiting the two-hole cabochon, pick up an 11º, a magatama, and an 11º, and sew through the adjacent hole in the cabochon with the needle pointing in the other direction **(photo v)**. Repeat step 1 on the other side of the cabochon.

2. Sew through the beadwork and work as in step 1 to embellish each cabochon.

Clasp

1. With the thread exiting the outermost set of holes in the end two-hole cabochon, pick up five 11ºs, and sew through the cabochon again in the same direction **(photo w)**. These beads will form a ring around the end of the cabochon. Continue through the first three 11ºs.

2. Pick up seven 15ºs and sew back through the 11º your thread exited at the start of this step to form a loop **(photo x)**. Retrace the thread path several times to secure, tying a couple of half-hitch knots between the beads (Basics).

3. Open a 4mm jump ring and attach one half of the clasp and the seven-bead loop (Basics). Close the ring.

4. Thread a needle on the tail and repeat steps 2 and 3 on the other end of the bracelet with the other half of the clasp. End the threads.

5. Open a 4mm jump ring and attach the seven-bead loop at the remaining end of the bracelet and one half of the clasp. Close the ring.

Romantic Interlude Necklace

This project combines a number of techniques to create an elegant necklace. You'll make bezeled stones, join components, weave tubular herringbone with "bubbles," and use just a touch of right-angle weave. Fussy details like the shaped connectors and the bubbles in the neck strap ratchet your beadwork up a couple of notches. If you can't wait to wear your creation, forgo the neck straps for now and attach a jump ring and a length of chain to each bowtie connector on either side of the assembled centerpiece. You can always add the neck straps later when you have more time.

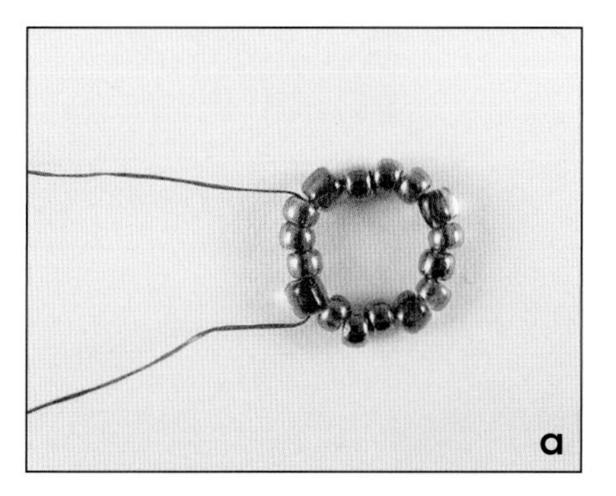

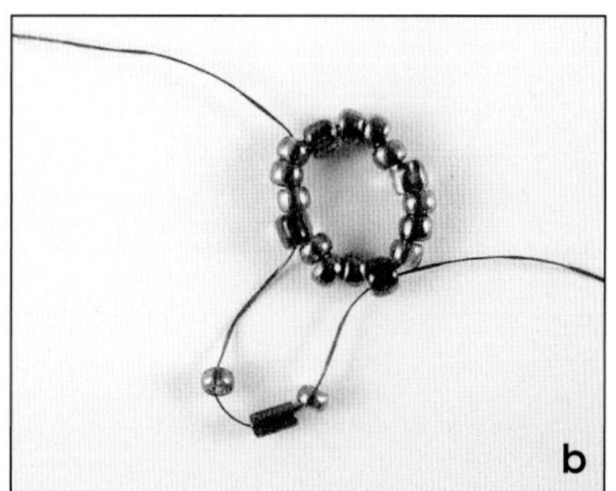

SUPPLIES

- **4** 8.2mm Swarovski crystal 1088-SS39 chaton stones
- **2** 6mm round glass beads
- 2g 3mm bugle beads (#1)
- 3g 2.8mm drop beads
- 1–2g 10º triangle seed beads
- 11º seed beads, 3g color A, 4g each of colors B and C
- **10** 15º seed beads
- Clasp
- Beading needle, #11
- Fireline, 6 lb. test

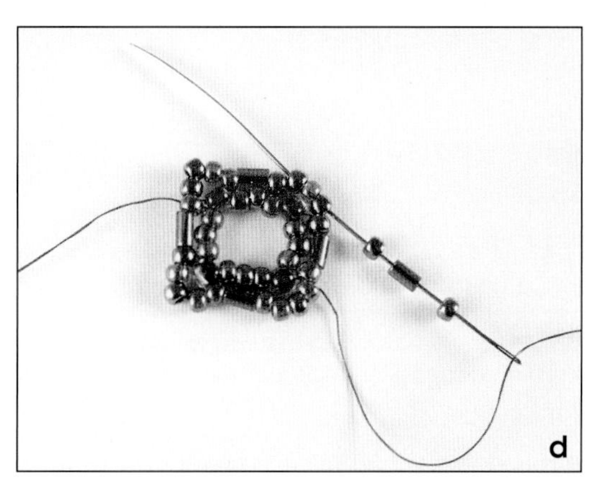

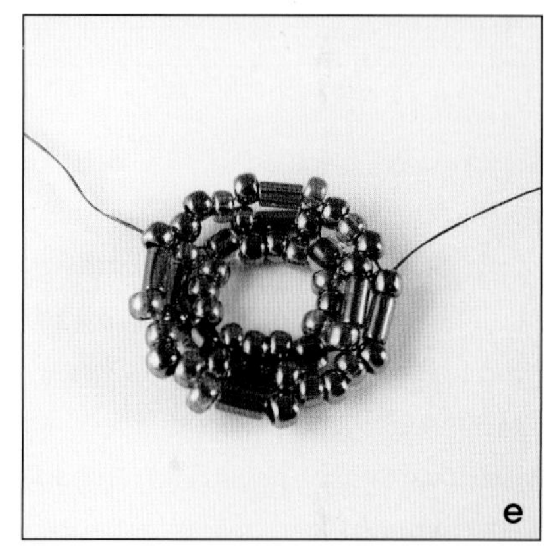

Bezeled Stone Components

1. Thread a needle on 2 ft. (1.8m) of thread. Pick up a repeating pattern of three color A 11º seed beads and a 10º triangle seed bead for a total of four triangles, leaving a 6-in. (15cm) tail. Tie a square knot with the tail to form a ring. Retrace the thread path and exit a triangle **(photo a)**.

2. Pick up an A, a 3mm bugle bead, and an A. Skip the three As in the original ring, and sew through the next triangle **(photo b)**. Repeat this stitch to complete the round, and step up through the first A, bugle, and A added in this round.

3. Pick up three As and sew through the next A, bugle, and A added in the previous round **(photo c)**. Repeat to complete the round, and step up through the first three As added in this round.

4. Pick up an A, a bugle, and an A, and sew through the next three-bead set added in the previous round **(photo d)**. Repeat to complete the round, using a firm tension so the beadwork begins to cup slightly. Step up through the first A, bugle, and A added in this step **(photo e)**.

f

g

h

i

j

5. Pick up a triangle, and sew through the next A, bugle, and A added in the previous round **(photo f)**. Snug up the beadwork. Insert the SS39 chaton stone face down into the beadwork **(photo g)**, and hold it in place with your thumb while you stitch. Repeat the first stitch in this step to complete the round, using a firm tension to secure the stone in the bezel. Step up through the first triangle added in this step **(photo h)**.

6. Pick up three As, and sew through the next triangle added in the previous round, and snug up the beads. Repeat to complete the round, then retrace the thread path through the beads in this round, tying a couple of half-hitch knots between the beads (Basics, p. 12), and end the tail, but not the working thread (Basics). Set the bezeled stone aside.

tip

When you add each triangle bead, pull the thread snug so the three As added in step 3 pop out to form a corner.

tip

If you tend to stitch with looser tension, before ending your thread, sew through all the As added in the last round, skipping the triangle beads.

7. Work as in steps 1–6 to create three more bezeled stones.

Twisted Herringbone Rope

To give the rope just a bit more interest, I mixed together bronze, light bronze, and gold luster 11º seed beads (A, B, and C). In these instructions, I refer to the beads in this mixture as 11ºs. You can use a single color if you choose.

1. Thread a needle on a comfortable length of thread. Pick up four 11º seed beads and sew through the beads again to form a ring, leaving an 8-in. (20cm) tail. Continue through the first three 11ºs, and pick up a 6mm round bead **(photo i)**.

2. Pick up four 11ºs and sew through these four beads again, pushing this ring down close to the 6mm, and continue through the first two 11ºs in this new ring **(photo j)**. Sew down through the 6mm and the 11º the tail is exiting **(photo k)**.

3. Sew through the 6mm and then sew through one of the 11ºs on this side of the 6mm **(photo l)**.

4. Pick up two 11ºs, and sew through the next two 11ºs in the ring on this side of the pearl. Pick up two 11ºs, sew through the next two 11ºs in

the original ring, and step up through the first 11º added in this step **(photo m)**.

5. Pick up two 11ºs, and sew down through the next 11º in the adjacent column. Skip the next 11º, sew through the following two 11ºs **(photo n)**, and snug up the threads.

6. Pick up two 11ºs, and sew down through the 11º in the next column and sew up through the last two 11ºs in the next column **(photo o)**. Snug up the beads. This will pull both sides of the beadwork up to begin to form a tube of four columns of beads **(photo p)**.

7. Work as in steps 5 and 6 until you have 20 beads in each column, ending and adding thread as needed.

8. Create a "bubble": Work as in steps 5 and 6, picking up 2.8mm drop beads in place of 11ºs.

9. Work as in steps 5 and 6 until you have 15 11ºs after the drop bead in each column, ending and adding thread as needed.

10. Continue working as in steps 8–10 until you have five "bubbles." Then work as in steps 5 and 6 until you have six 11ºs after the drop beads in each column.

11. Pick up an 11º, and sew down through the 11º in the next column and up through the 11º in the following column. Pick up an 11º and sew down through the 11º in the next column and up through the 11º in the following column and continue through the first 11º picked up in this step.

12. Pick up five 15º seed beads and half of the clasp, and sew through the second 11º added in the previous step, and then sew through the first 11º added in the previous step. Retrace the thread path several times to secure, and end the working thread.

13. Make a second neck strap.

q

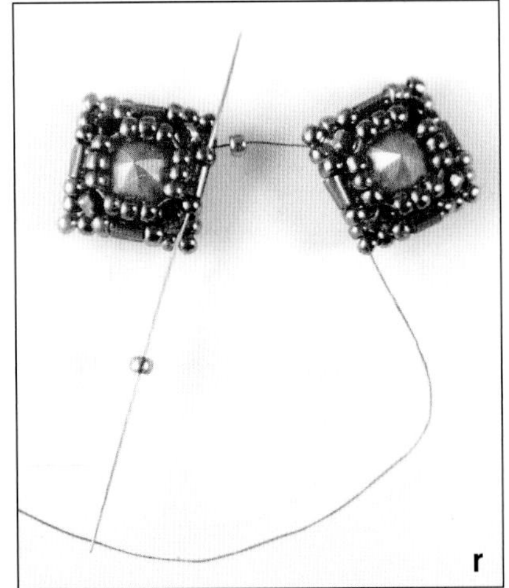
r

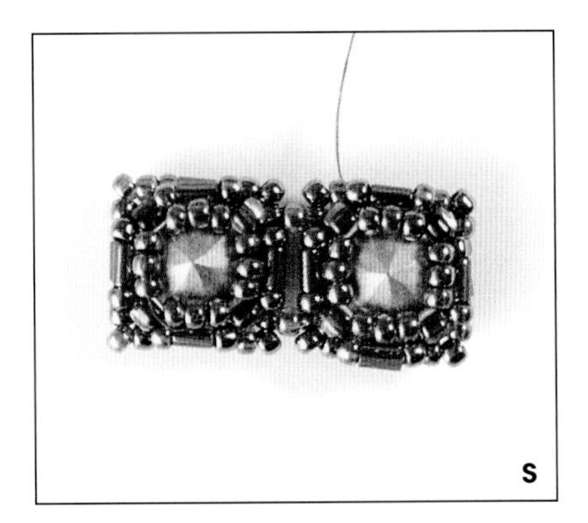
s

t

Centerpiece

1. Thread a needle on the working thread of one of the bezeled stones, and working on the back of the stone, sew through the beadwork to exit an A, bugle, and A.

2. Pick up an A, and sew through the corresponding A, bugle, and A on the back of a second bezeled stone **(photo q)**. Pick up an A, and sew through the A, bugle, and A your thread exited at the start of this step **(photo r)**, and snug up the beads. Retrace the thread path through the beads in this step several times to secure. Then sew through the beadwork on the back of the second bezeled stone to exit the A, bugle, and A on the side adjacent to the join just created **(photo s)**.

3. Work as in step 2 to join a third bezeled stone component. Sew through the beadwork to exit the corner A in the center bezeled stone component **(photo t)**.

4. Sew through the nearest corner A on the adjacent component, pick up an A, a triangle, and an A, sew through the corner A on the third component, and sew through the A your thread exited at the start of this step. Retrace the thread path using a firm tension and end the thread.

5. Thread a needle on the working thread on the fourth bezeled stone component, and sew through the beadwork to exit a corner A.

6. Pick up an A, and sew through the corresponding corner A on the center bezeled stone component as show in **photo u**. Pick up an A, and sew through the A your thread exited at the start of this step. Retrace the thread path several times to secure and end the thread.

Bowtie Connector

1. Thread a needle on a comfortable length of thread. Pick up nine As, and sew through all the beads again to form a ring, leaving a 6-in. (15cm) tail. Continue through the first two As.

2. Skip the next A, sew through the following two As, and snug up the beads so the skipped A pops out. Repeat twice. Sew through the nearest popped out A.

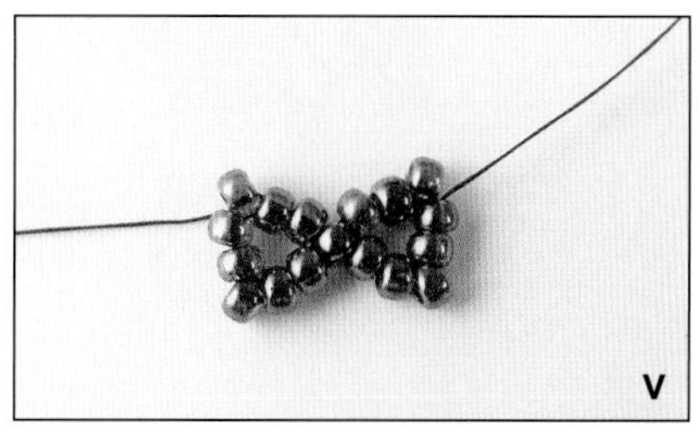

Designer's Note

Replace each triangle bead in step 1 with a 3mm bicone crystal for added sparkle.

3. Pick up eight As and sew through the A your thread exited at the start of this step to form a ring.

4. Work as in step 2 to create a bowtie shape. Sew through the beadwork to exit the two beads opposite the shared A **(photo v)**.

5. Pick up an A and sew through the A, bugle, and A on the outer edge of the centerpiece as shown in **photo w**. Pick up an A, and sew through the two As in the bowtie your thread exited at the start of this step. Retrace the thread path several times. Then sew through the beadwork on the bowtie to exit the two As on the opposite side of the bowtie.

6. Work as in step 5 to connect the end of the bowtie to the A, bugle, and A on the back of the same bezeled stone, gentle folding the beadwork at the shared A. Sew through the beadwork to exit the shared A **(photo x)**. End the tail, but not the working thread.

7. Sew up through the center of the four-bead ring at the end of a neck strap, the 6mm, and one of the 11°s in the ring at the top of the 6mm. Sew down through an adjacent 11°, the 6mm, the center of the four bead ring, and through the A your thread exited at the start of this step. Retrace the thread path several times and end the thread **(photo y)**.

8. Work as in steps 1–7 to create another bowtie connector and connect the remaining neck strap to the other side of the centerpiece.

Acknowledgments

Writing this book has been something I have dreamed about for many years, and without the love and support of so many people, it would not have been possible.

Many thanks to the following:

- My parents, the original DIY-ers, who taught me to teach myself how to make things by reading and following instructions.
- My sister Mary who supported my habit by selling my jewelry to her friends, co-workers, and acquaintances at her scrapbook weekends so I could buy more beads.
- My husband Anthony and my daughter Sophia, who allowed me to lock myself in the "bead room" (which used to be the den until my beads exploded!) for months and months on end.

- Erica (Swanson) Barse, editor at Kalmbach Books, whose calm, unruffled demeanor is as amazing as her ability to break things down into manageable pieces. I'm very glad to have had the opportunity to work with her on this project.
- Lisa Bergman, designer extraordinaire, whose work I love! I'm delighted to be able to work with Lisa again.
- Bill Zubak, who explained my lighting issues and cleaned up my not-so-great photos.

About the Author

Jane Danley Cruz was first introduced to beading when she was nine years old by her sister, Beth, who showed her how to crochet a Flapper-style necklace using tiny pearls. Since then, Jane has been fascinated with beads. By happenstance, on a trip to New York in 1992, she learned tubular peyote from a clerk at a bead store. While no one could have known it at the time, that trip was the start of a wonderful bead journey from which she has never looked back! Suddenly she became aware that lots of people were doing lots of interesting things with beads, and she was determined to master the many stitches and techniques associated with the art of beading. Since 1998, she has been designing original jewelry, writing instructions, and teaching classes.

In 2010, Jane moved from Chicago, Illinois to Waukesha, Wisconsin to work at *Bead&Button* magazine as an Associate Editor for both *Bead&Button* and *Wirework*. In addition, she occasionally worked as a contributing editor to *BeadStyle* magazine and a technical editor for several jewelry books published by Kalmbach Books.

In 2014, Jane moved back to the Chicago area with her husband and daughter, where she now works for a healthcare company. However, her passion for beading has not waivered and she takes time to bead almost every day as her own form of meditation and relaxation therapy. Her first book, *Dragons, Crystals & Chainmaille*, was published by Kalmbach in March of 2017 and is filled with mystical- and mythical-inspired projects.

Create Stunning Jewelry with Step-by-Step Project Books

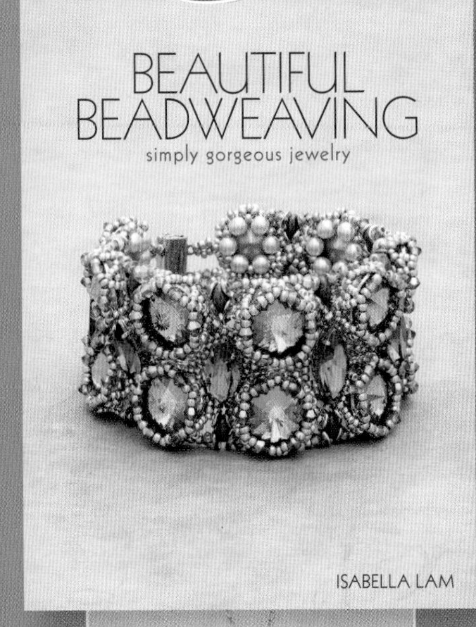

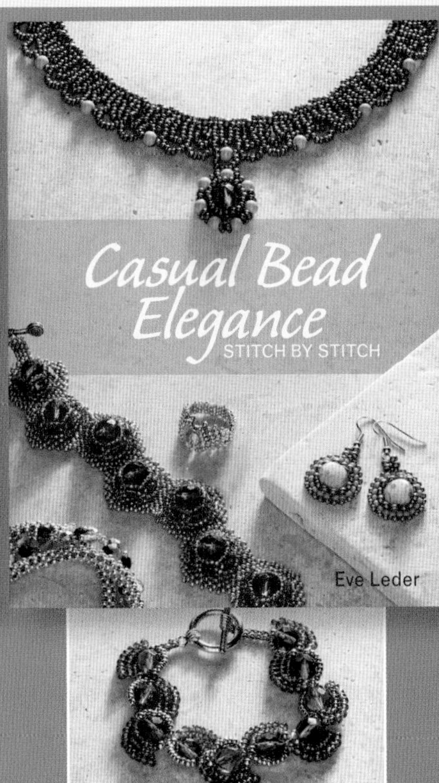

Beautiful Beadweaving: Simply Gorgeous Jewelry

25 exquisite projects that focus on creating detailed and striking stitched jewelry.

#67882 • $22.99

Learn to Use Two-Hole Beads with 20 Fabulous Projects

Creative projects for beautiful jewelry using two-hole bead techniques.

#67891 • $21.99

Casual Bead Elegance, Stitch by Stitch

24 gorgeous stitching projects in a wide variety of colors, styles, and skill levels.

#67884 • $22.99

Buy now from your favorite craft or bead shop!
Shop at JewelryandBeadingStore.com

P30544

Sales tax where applicable.